"A must read for anyone interested in succeeding in today's highly competitive, global business environment. John Rehfeld clearly articulates why the best way is not OUR way or THEIR way but an intelligent combination of the two."

Edward M. Esber, Jr.
President and CEO
Creative Labs, Inc.

"No serious manager can afford to skip John Rehfeld's new book. It stands head and shoulders above others by offering immediately usable practical advice backed up by impeccable analysis. Among the very few Americans to become a member of senior management in two major Japanese corporations, Mr. Rehfeld is the consummate insider—and a superb writer."

Dr. Hiroki Kato
Vice President, Asia
IMOGA Corporation

"There is the Western Management style and of course the Japanese. John Rehfeld after spending years as a senior executive working for Japanese companies has evolved a better way which combines the best of both styles. As companies continue to globalize, the search for a 'world management style' will continue. What may well emerge is something along the lines suggested in *Alchemy of a Leader*."

Dennis Laurie, PhD
The Peter F. Drucker Graduate Management Center
Claremont Graduate School

"John Rehfeld has been there. He's been a successful leader in both Western and Japanese management cultures. Because he speaks from his experience and his heart, *Alchemy of a Leader* offers a practical, real world tested recipe for combining the best of Western and Japanese management methods."

David Dibble
Creator of the TQM Leadership Experience

"*Alchemy of a Leader* is for real: a delight to read and filled with just plain good stuff. It is experience and wisdom, shared. It contains wisdom born out of the hard crucible of real experience. John Rehfeld provides a fantastic learning experience on how to do things better."

Walter F. Beran
Ernst & Young

"Executives and managers will never have a better opportunity to get an inside and in-depth look at Japanese business skills. John's book combines real experience with extensive research to provide a unique understanding of the heritage and tradition behind how and why the Japanese perform their jobs in the unrelenting manner of 'Kaizen'."

William P. Conlin
President
CalComp, A Lockheed Company

". . . John Rehfeld is a proven master of combining the management techniques of both Japan and the West to produce exceptional results."

Rod Hosilyk
Computer Products Plus, Inc.

"Full of practical and useful advice that can be applied immediately. Unlike other books that either praise or criticize the Japanese management style, *Alchemy of a Leader* methodically crafts together Japanese best practices with Western best practices to create an unbeatable combination."

Phil Baker
Apple Computer

"For someone who thought there was very little left to discover about Japanese business style, I learned a great deal from this book."

Mark E. Thomas
President and CEO
Standard Communications

"Rehfeld's significant experience within Toshiba and Seiko Instruments, his role in helping to build the laptop computer industry in the U.S., coupled with his keen interest in applying lessons of other cultures— especially Japan—to improve his company's results, have given him a novel laboratory in which to perform tests, assess results, perform more tests, and learn in a real setting what works and what does not."

Steven C. Clemons
Executive Director
Institute for Independent Japanese Companies
Immediate Past Executive Director
Japan America Society of Southern California

"If the requirements for writing a book are experience, deep reflection, creative insights and love of the subject, then John Rehfeld eminently qualifies. In *Alchemy of a Leader* John has written a practical, readable and visionary book for Westerners and Japanese who interface in the workplace and the marketplace."

Hugh Leonard
Leonard Training and Consulting

"Considering myself well-read in management theory, I've encountered many of the ideas put forth by John Rehfeld before, however, the practical and forthright nature of his presentation creates an imperative I have not yet encountered."

Bradford F. Spencer, PhD
Principal, Spencer/Shenk & Associates, Inc.

aLCHEMY
of a
LEADER

aLCHEMY
of a
LEADER

Combining Western and Japanese Management Skills to Transform Your Company

JOHN E. REHFELD

JOHN WILEY & SONS, INC.
New York · Chichester · Brisbane ·
Toronto · Singapore

Copyright © 1994 by John E. Rehfeld

Published by John Wiley & Sons, Inc.
All rights reserved. Published simultaneously in Canada.

Library of Congress Cataloging-in-Publication Data:

Rehfeld, John E., 1940–
    Alchemy of a leader : combining western and Japanese
management skills to transform your company / John E. Rehfeld.
        p.   cm.
    Includes index.
    ISBN 0-471-00836-2 (cloth)
    1. Industrial management.   I. Title.
HD70.U5R45   1994
658—dc20   93-34342

Printed in the United States of America

10 9 8 7 6 5 4 3 2 1

Dedicated to my Mother
and my recently departed Father

CONTENTS

Contents

Acknowledgments

Like most effective endeavors, writing this book was a collaborative effort. I owe a great debt to the many individuals and organizations who invested themselves in this book's successful completion. First and foremost among these was my gifted and experienced editorial consultant, Hal Plotkin, who helped me focus my ideas and worked with me to find the right words to express them.

Those who generously aided in my understanding and testing of Japanese business practices have also earned my everlasting gratitude. While it is impossible to thank everyone who helped, several people simply cannot be omitted. Among these are former Seiko Instruments colleagues, Vice Chairman Dr. Hara, President K. Itoh, Seiko Instruments, USA Chairman, H. Fukino, and other Seiko Instrument's employees including Junichi Hattori, Scott Maeda, K. Watanabe, and Hiro Motoshima. Former Toshiba colleagues

Shay Takeuchi, K. Hataya, K. Ishiguro, Mark Tanaka, Yoshi Maeda, and T. Hirai gave me an early opportunity to use Japanese management techniques. Also Aki Tsurakame, Yoshi Noguchi, Hideko Ishisaki Harris, H. Takematsu, Keiko Kimura, Hugh Leonard, Darian Kennedy, Yugi Ogino, Keiko Kitta, Steve Clemmons, and Fujitsu's former FDK America president, talented and gracious Mr. Kuramoto, gave me more understanding of the two business cultures.

I was also fortunate to have several key literary mentors who encouraged my efforts early on and sustained me with their faith and confidence. At *Harvard Business Review,* Geri Willigan gave this book an important jump-start by publishing an early version of this material in the *Harvard Business Review.* Similarly, support from Spenser Johnson, Bill Ouchi, Tom Peters, Kenichi Ohmae, and Hiroki Kato also made valuable contributions by sharing their expertise as accomplished authors and business scholars. Finally, I must also thank Pepperdine University Senior Fellow Joel Kotkin, whose introductions to his colleagues provided critical logistical support.

A number of other individuals assisted enormously by encouraging me, and reviewing and critiquing manuscript drafts. Their varied perspectives helped me refine my arguments and gave me the opportunity to have my work tested and challenged, prior to publication, by some of the best minds I know. I'm certain this book would not have come to its fullest fruition were it not for the efforts and encouragement of Brad Spenser, Tom Shenk, Lisbet Thoresen, Kenny Slutsky, Rod Hosilyk, Jeff Weiss, and Bob Kelly of So Cal Ten. Also, I thank former Seiko Instruments colleague Lynn Keyser, Lenore Arce, and my YPO forum group for their extraordinary support.

I also relied on several organizations for research and editorial support during the writing of this book. These organizations include the USC IBEAR program, the Aspen

Institute–Japan/Western Seminar, Northwestern University's School of Business, and the Southern California Japan-American Society, so ably led by its chairman, Walter Beran. Each of these organizations is actively involved in building the cultural and economic bridges that offer the best hope for a more harmonious and prosperous world. I was honored to have their assistance.

I must thank my talented editor at John Wiley and Sons, John Mahaney, as well as his colleagues, Joan O'Neil and publisher Karl Weber, for so quickly grasping the value of this work and helping me emphasize the theme that global management, in the final analysis, is really all about effective leadership.

Finally, I thank my wife Gunvor and my children for their enduring patience, love, and support during this project.

aLCHEMY
of a
LEADER

INTRODUCTION: The Twenty-first-Century Alchemist

Like other people, managers in today's business world are products of their own culture. They've learned ways of solving problems, communicating with others, organizing their work, and making decisions that are deeply influenced by the folkways of the society in which they grew up. There's nothing wrong with this—in fact, it's completely natural and normal. But in today's globally competitive and interdependent business world, culture-bound management skills are no longer good enough.

To be effective, today's manager must be a kind of "business alchemist." Alchemy can be defined as the art of transforming something common into something special. The twenty-first-century alchemist will absorb business methods and knowledge from many cultures and transform them into new skills needed to compete in the new global marketplace. The purpose of *Alchemy of a Leader* is to show how this can be done.

My career has provided me with a unique opportunity to be a management alchemist by observing what works and what doesn't in two very different business cultures. For 12 years I was one of the few Westerners to hold senior management positions in two major Japanese companies. I was able to use this experience as a research laboratory of sorts. First, as vice president and general manager at the computer division Toshiba America, where I led the team that built Toshiba's

1

lap-top business from zero to $350 million in less than a decade and, more recently, as president of Seiko Instruments, USA, I've discovered how to improve the Western management style by combining it with some very specific Japanese techniques. In addition, as a member of a variety of senior-level management groups such as the Young President's organization, SOCALTEN (a southern California high-tech CEO roundtable), and several southern California high-tech company boards, I've kept my Western perspective fresh. Combined with my earliest business experience at leading American global companies such as Arthur D. Little, International Data Corporation, IBM, and ITT, this background helped me harmoniously blend successful Western and Japanese management practices. Most recently my research laboratory has come full circle. In my new role as president and CEO of Etak, Inc., part of Rupert Murdoch's News Corporation, I've been able to test my alchemist ideas in a very Western business environment.

These combined management skills work! Armed with an understanding of the strengths of both Western and Japanese management styles, I'm now able to share with readers what I've learned. There are literally dozens of specific effective management skills I've derived by combining the most successful Japanese and Western approaches, fine tuning what works, and discarding what does not work. Nearly all of these techniques can be applied right away by individuals and by companies seeking to compete more effectively. However, making these changes won't be easy. Most of them require crucial, yet subtle, changes in personal orientation and at least some appreciation of the role culture plays in business.

This book is designed to help make these changes. As a manager for the past 20 years, I've read most of the previously published books on both Japanese and Western business practices. Nearly all of them were penned by academicians, consultants, and journalists rather than people with more practical line management experience. Unfortunately, most of the recommendations contained in these books can't be implemented by people like me—managers attempting to solve problems now.

As a working line manager I've also been in a position to try and see how both Japanese and Western management techniques work in practice. What's in this book works in the business environment of the 1990s. I've discarded many of the hot ideas of the past few years that don't hack it in today's rapidly evolving global business world. For example, many managers during the 1980s imported Japanese consensus management, myself included. What they—and I—found is that it takes too long and doesn't work effectively. Neither does Western-style top-down authoritarian management. What I've synthesized from these two business cultures is a collaborative management style, something that's neither totally Western nor totally Japanese but uniquely suited to today's global business world.

Alchemy of a Leader was created for managers, entrepreneurs, and beleaguered workers. Its first message is that success in global business has little to do with whether a company is Japanese, North American, or European, and everything to do with some tried and true professional techniques.

Alchemy's second message is that by understanding the cultural foundations of business management practices, both in the West and in Japan, we can more closely examine the role culture plays in determining our economic prosperity. It is possible, I've learned, to benefit from the best of both worlds by combining and adapting proven Japanese management techniques with attitudes and approaches more common in our own western society.

The perspective taken in these pages is that of a businessperson, not a historian, sociologist, psychologist, cultural anthropologist, or economist. Nonetheless, in seeking to understand modern business management techniques I've had to learn something of the history, culture, sociology, anthropology, and psychology that shapes these activities. Of course, I make no claims regarding the scholarly or scientific discipline used in formulating my perspective on either the Japanese or Western culture. As a businessman, I'm merely interested in what works.

Japanese and Western societies are in many ways quite dissimilar. For example, people in the West tend to emphasize individualism and direct communications while most Japanese prefer a group orientation and a more restrained style of indirect interpersonal communications. Many scholars contend that these differences are attributable to the historical and geographical forces that shaped a wildly divergent sense of the collective unconscious in Japan and in the West.

The "open frontier" in the formative period of the heterogeneous American culture stands in stark contrast to the homogeneous, rice-farming society that developed on the isolated island that is Japan. These divergent societal backgrounds greatly influence modern management styles. Although it is vital to understand some of this history, the main focus of this book is on the present, and on what can be learned from these different management styles and what can be applied in our own lives today.

Similarly, the long-standing trade debate raging between Tokyo on the one hand and Washington, Toronto, London, and Bonn on the other which helped give rise to this book, is also not central to my effort put on these pages. I'm often asked, "Why do Japanese companies succeed in the global market?" My standard reply: (A) because of a strong government-industrial policy; (B) "unfair" trade practices that often resemble American antitrust violations; and (C) some truly excellent management techniques.

This book deals with "C," primarily because "A" and "B"

are beyond the scope of influence of the average Western manager or worker. This is not to minimize the importance of Japanese governmental, financial, or trading policies or the relationship of these practices to the trade friction between Japan and much of the rest of the world.

However, if we place successful, proven, and practical management tools in the hands of those who can use them—line managers and workers—we can no doubt improve the performance of those managers and their businesses. I'm prepared to leave the debate about macroeconomic policies and international trade regulations to the politicians, economists, and journalists. Meanwhile, we workers and managers have some serious work to do.

Japanese business leaders who successfully merged Western business techniques with their own unique cultural assets after World War II demonstrated that a country's economic culture can change over time. Western managers now have a similar strategic opportunity that goes far beyond the day-to-day application of the techniques reviewed in this book. Without swallowing our pride or abandoning the best parts of our own varied nationalities we now have the power to create in our workplaces an entirely new culture, one that is neither fully Japanese nor fully Western, but rather a combination of the two. The development of this new business culture, which draws its strength from the most successful management techniques from the West and from Japan, is inevitable; the only question is where the next phase of this ongoing evolution will unfold. Like Japanese business leaders and managers did earlier in the century, today's hard-pressed managers now have the opportunity to turn the challenges they confront into opportunities.

Today's marketplace is global, whether you are a manager in a Fortune 500 corporation or in a much smaller operation. There is no *one* best way to manage. There is only learning from and adopting the best techniques, just as the

Japanese did almost fifty years ago. It's my hope that *Alchemy of a Leader* contributes to you and your company being a global success.

By combining successful Japanese management techniques with basic Western sensibilities of fair play, and respect for women, acceptance of outsiders and for the freedom and potential of the individual, our businesses can return to a position of global preeminence. Nurturing the growth and development of this new hybrid managerial attitude is the primary goal of this book.

1

JULIUS CAESAR'S GHOST:

Rethinking Time and Budget Cycles

What did Julius Caesar know about managing a modern company? Not much, obviously. Today, Rome is primarily a tourist attraction. Nonetheless, Caesar's most enduring creation, his 12-month Julian calendar, continues to influence the way many modern companies are managed, or, more properly, mismanaged. Managers can profitably apply the leader's alchemy through some simple yet extremely effective techniques for analyzing time and budgets.

The impact of Caesar's 12-month calendar on business is so obvious it is usually overlooked. It often hangs like an invisible millstone around a manager's neck, doing little to enhance company performance while providing a business schedule that not only allows but can actually foster debilitating setbacks.

In current practice, the 12-month Julian calendar remains the most commonly used measuring stick applied to business performance over time. It is worth noting, however, that the 12-month calendar has virtually nothing, historically speaking, to do with business—excluding, of course, Rome's penchant for taxation on a regular and predictable schedule. Instead, the 12-month calendar exists because that is roughly how long it takes for the earth to make one full revolution around the sun.

That's nice. However, as I've learned from my Japanese colleagues, the 12-month calendar affords no special advantages when it comes to developing, implementing, and monitoring business plans or identifying variances to budgets and putting in place plans to fix those variances. Nonetheless, most businesspeople, at least those outside Japan, seem to march lockstep to the beat of a 12-month business calendar. Understanding how and why this occurs can lead managers to more effective business scheduling and monitoring practices.

What Time Is It, Anyway?

Former Northwestern University professor Hiroki Kato has observed that just as the Japanese use a different form of nonlinear, circular logic in their decision-making, they also have a very different conception of time itself. In addition to its influence on the decision-making process, this different sense of time affects the mechanics of budgeting, forecasting, and planning.

Along with a handful of other leading Japanese scholars, Professor Kato has settled on a name for this phenomenon; the Japanese, he says, are a polychronic people while Americans and other Westerners tend to be more monochronic. Monochronic refers to paying attention to and only doing one thing at a time, while polychronic means being involved with many things simultaneously.

The 12-month calendar is like a time map for a monochronic person. The polychronic person, on the other hand, doesn't need or want a time map that may be unrelated to overall objectives. Experience in different countries leads me to the conclusion that, as a general rule, polychronic attitudes prevail in the Arab world, some Mediterranean countries, and Japan. Monochronic sensibilities, again as a general rule, tend to dominate most businesses in the United States, Canada, Scandinavia, and Northern Europe.

In monochronic cultures and systems, time is everything, and the schedule—the calendar—can become more important than anything else, becoming virtually sacred and unalterable. Sociologists maintain that the Western monochronic orientation grew in part out of the industrial revolution, which enforced rigid schedules on Northern European factory workers.

Polychronic time, on the other hand, is characterized by the simultaneous occurrence of many things, by a great degree of involvement with other people, and by schedules that are dictated according to the requirements of the situation. In a polychronic culture, there is more emphasis on completing human transactions in the most productive manner rather than holding to some predetermined schedule. For example, two classically polychronic businesspeople conversing on a street corner would likely opt to be late for their next appointments rather than abruptly terminate a conversation, choosing instead to bring the discussion to its natural conclusion.

The modern Japanese have combined their indigenous polychronic approach with the Western monochronic system of time management. In their dealings with foreigners and in their use of technology, the Japanese are quite monochronic. However, when it comes to important decisions, like budgeting and planning, or their personal relationships, most Japanese tend to be entirely polychronic.

The Japanese conception of time explains why organizations in Japan rarely become prisoners of Julius Caesar's system of time measurement, as frequently happens in the West. The 12-month time frame is of little practical value, whether introducing a new product to market, developing and training a sales force, generating feedback from customers, establishing a new division, or monitoring corporate performance, except for helping us get to meetings on the right day. The earth has its cycles around the sun and in today's fast-paced global environment, business also has its cycles. But they are not the same.

Budget for Six Months

My Japanese managers at Toshiba were the first to introduce me to this different and, in many cases, more effective system of time management. Upon arriving at Toshiba, I immediately had to adjust to the customary Japanese six-month budgeting cycle. In recent years, so much attention has been paid by the Western business press to the Japanese fixation with long-term planning it may surprise some to learn that, in a polychronistic way, the best Japanese managers are usually as focused on the next week as they are on the next decade. The typical Japanese budgeting and planning system helps reinforce this careful blend of long-term planning and short-term business generalship.

The Japanese budgeting process is typically very disciplined. Owing to their culture's polychronic sensibilities, it is also quite different. In Japan, the fiscal year generally runs from April through March. Usually, a full-year budget is prepared in February and March. However, only the first six months, called the "A" period, are approved. The "B" part, the second six months, is then modified based on the initial results in the "A" period and gains formal approval sometime in August or September.

Like any other western businessperson, I arrived at Toshiba with a 12-month mind-set, so the budgeting periods seemed, at first, to come up much too fast. I had no sooner developed a budget and countermeasures to correct variances than I found myself doing it all over again. I was also forced to give employee performance reviews and set Manager's Bonus Objectives (MBOs) twice as often.

Six-month budgeting seemed, initially, like an officious and needlessly redundant management activity. But after three or four fiscal periods, I began to clearly see the power of the process. Eventually, I discovered that six-month budgeting is one of the most powerful Japanese management techniques that can be applied in western businesses.

Over the years, I've learned to welcome the opportunity to change my budgets more frequently, in part because the world, particularly the high-tech world, changes so much in six months. Having two deadlines each year leaves less room for procrastination, especially the well-intended routine kind that is often tied to adherence to a rigid annual plan. If you are slipping from the budget after the first quarter and you know have only three months instead of nine months to get back on target, you naturally work that much harder to figure out what to do. A greater sense of urgency is created.

For example, in many businesses the Christmas buying season drives important management decisions, such as appropriate production levels, inventory, and personnel needs. In February, however, it is hard to focus on these needs for the following holiday season, especially if you are operating within a 12-month budget. However, if your budget period ends a month or two before the winter buying rush, it allows seasonal needs to be anticipated closer to their actual occurrence. This helps put a company's targets within range and provides more realistic appraisals of any looming or potential problems.

Six-month budgeting can play an important role in overall corporate performance, particularly in the sales and marketing arenas. Most executives responsible for these areas are already aware of the "hockey stick" effect—the tendency

11

of sales activities to increase dramatically as a budget or sales monitoring period comes to an end.

"Hockey stick," of course, refers to the angle of the sales or profit line on an employee or division performance graph. Usually, in any given year, monthly sales reports show a fairly straight-line progression up until the 11th month. Then, in most cases, excluding those of failing businesses, there is often a sharp turn upwards. This comes about because of the extra effort made to beat the clock, meet the deadline, and close sales.

Given these realities, the line on an annual sales monitoring chart often looks like a hockey stick, with the initial months forming the handle and the final month forming the blade. Budgeting for six months instead of 12 is a valuable technique because it provides the opportunity to have two hockey sticks each year instead of one. This, presumably, leads to more overall sales and profits.

Of course, many non-Japanese companies, North American and European firms included, already notice hockey stick results at the end of their fiscal quarters. However, there is no hockey stick like that which results at the end of a final budget period. While virtually all companies keep a close eye on quarterly results, few Western companies take this practice to its logical conclusion and award bonuses based on quarterly or half-year results. In Japan, in contrast, MBOs are set in the six-month time frame and the end of a six-month budget period is considered to be an endpoint rather than a kind of half- or midway marker.

Additionally, budgets are usually a manager's most vital planning tool. If, due to unforeseen circumstances, a 12-month budget becomes meaningless during the course of a year, a company can become like a ship without a rudder. If you are running a company with several divisions, the cumulative effect of variances to a number of one-year budgets can be quite devastating. Three divisions, each off by 20%, can leave senior executives with massive year-end problems.

Six-month budgets, on the other hand, create a far greater sense of urgency; problem areas are noted sooner and remedial strategies can be implemented more quickly, leaving managers with more control of the overall situation.

In business, there are few things as final as a budget. Most companies, of course, already generate quarterly budget forecasts, alternative budgets, and revised budgets. However, in reality, there is usually only one implemented budget. In most Western corporations, it is typically a yearly budget broken into co-equal quarters. In fact, when working with Westerners I always have to make certain we agree on a common budget vocabulary. The budget is what commissions are paid on; it is what Manager's Bonus Objectives (MBOs) are based on; and it represents the final commitment of the board management to a company. Budget forecasts and budget revisions are not new budgets; they are variances to an original budget. With a 12-month budget, there are necessarily many such revisions. In this environment, it is very easy to lose track of what the original budget commitment was and what changes have occurred or are occurring.

Additionally, each new budget provides a chance to wipe the slate clean and start over, which helps motivate managers and workers by allowing them to bring goals into line with objective and demonstrated measures of reality. All managers miss their budgets from time to time, especially if they are the typically ambitious budgets found in most growth-minded companies. But if a manager slips so much off budget that he or she loses hope of ever hitting the target, motivation can also be lost. If employees know they don't stand a chance of meeting their budget objectives, the tendency is to give up and start making excuses.

For example, when I joined Seiko Instruments, USA, where 98% of the employees are Americans, its seven divisions were using a Western-style 12-month budget cycle. One of the computer peripherals divisions at the company, which is in a particularly volatile industry, was so far off the plan that managers were not even referring to the original budget. They had given up on it and instead were putting up a new set of numbers on the wall every month. They spent virtually no time at all concentrating on developing and implementing the countermeasures required to minimize the negative variances to their own original budget.

Since then, all Seiko Instruments, USA divisions have switched to a six-month budget. It took about a year and a half for people to get used to the new system, but it seems to be working. Last year, the same peripherals division was off budget again, but it was off for three months instead of ten. Knowing that the end of the fiscal period was just three months away, the division managers immediately developed countermeasures to minimize the variances to their budget. Midyear, they reset the budget and came up with still more countermeasures.

If they had still been using the 12-month budget, this division would have been directionless for months, foiled by Julius Caesar. However, by stopping to ask why they were off and then making the necessary adjustments, they put a rudder on their ship. The division, formerly in the red by about 30%, finished the year about 10% off target, but that number is something managers can get their arms around and fix in the next six-month period. Six-month budgeting provides a business schedule that is generally more conducive to the kind of hands-on, market-oriented management style now required in most competitive businesses. For that reason, bonuses and other special commissions paid on a six-month schedule have a much more invigorating impact than does a year-end bonus.

When I tell my non-Japanese peers about six-month budgeting I'm often told they'd find it impossible to work within this short time frame. In many cases, the business budgeting process is so cumbersome it can sometimes take an entire year to complete. One American manager made the revealing remark that if he had to create a new budget every six months it would "force some efficiencies into the budgeting process." Exactly.

Major budget targets are usually set fairly early in a budget planning process, which leads to variances that can grow in size as the budget period lengthens. If, for example, you take six months to develop a budget for the following 12 months, at the end of that budget period the figures you started with are a full 18 months old. In addition, the budgeting process usually expands to fill the amount of time allowed. It is quite ironic, then, that the more time allowed for budgeting the more likely it is that budget figures will be off target.

If, on the other hand, you take one to two months to develop a six-month budget you are never more than eight months away from the point at which you set your initial budget targets. That way, you keep the horse under you and the reins tightly in your hands.

I'm often asked if shortening the budget period is desirable, why not go to a quarterly plan? I've tried this approach and have discovered that it doesn't work as well. A quarter is usually too short a time period to make anything new or worthwhile happen. It is virtually impossible, in three short months, to create, approve, and communicate a new plan to all concerned when you have to start performing against another new plan every 90 days. Six months is, in practice, the most effective compromise. It ensures that a budget is realistic without consuming all of your time with the budget process. Having lived with it for more than a decade, six months feels just about right.

Frequent Performance Feedback

The sense of urgency created by the six-month budget process is also helpful in a variety of other business management tasks. For example, this shorter budget time frame encourages managers to sit down with subordinates and supervisors for more frequent, regularly scheduled, frank face-to-face performance reviews.

The yearly performance review, another holdover based on Julius Caesar's sense of time, is simply not good enough —especially in today's environment where a company can go from industry leader to industry goat in one short product cycle. In a single year, an area within one individual's responsibility can fall so far behind as to be practically irretrievable. I've seen it happen more than once. Increasing the frequency of employee performance reviews helps avoid this problem.

Providing at least one employee performance review every six months instead of once a year also turns out to be an excellent way of helping the process of work take on more of the satisfying character of play. Generally speaking, people do not like to work, but they do like to play. Interestingly, some fascinating recent research has revealed that one of the key differences between work and play involves the amount of immediate feedback participants receive.

If you think about it, many sports are quite monotonous and routine. Playing golf, for example, involves hitting the same ball over and over again (if you are lucky!), often in very familiar settings, with largely similar results over time. Many work tasks are like that. Yet golf is viewed as fun, while work is often seen as boring.

One of the key differences, researchers discovered, is that when playing, the feedback is certain and swift and a sense of challenge and reward is always present. In contrast, when working in a setting in which performance evaluations are done once a year the feedback is very slow and often imprecise. This leads to frustration and, sometimes, even a sense of futility.

More frequent performance feedback about work-related

issues can fill this void. Work can be made more fun and challenging through a pattern of increased regular, accurate performance measurements and reviews. This can be compared with the scorecard golfers fill out at the end of each hole. Given this rapid and specific scorecard-like feedback, I've even heard employees tell me, when faced with difficult work challenges, "Gee, this is kind of like a game." A comment like that is music in a manager's ears.

If employees expect yearly performance reviews and, for whatever reason, it becomes necessary to give one person more regular performance reviews, this can be perceived, by the group as well as by the concerned employee, to be an attack on that individual. Rather than improve performance, the expedited performance review can backfire, leading to grievances, charges of unfairness, and frenzied attempts at making excuses, rather than fixing the problem. Putting these exercises on a regular six-month schedule avoids this problem.

As an example, one Seiko Instruments, USA, employee was having severe performance problems until his manager sat down with him and developed very specific six-month work objectives. These specific objectives, along with the shorter time frame, allowed both the employee and the manager to monitor job performance closely and to step in and correct deficiencies promptly. In addition, the six-month time period led to the development of realistic productivity goals that both the employee and the manager regarded as reasonable. Somehow, goals pegged to a one-year time period often end up so wildly optimistic and unrealistic as to lead to later paralysis when they become what they really were from the start: unattainable.

By establishing the six-month cycle for all employees, a manager can keep tight reins on employees while maintaining the sense of managerial fairness and equity that enhances teamwork. It also reduces the magnitude of individual failures, helping maintain employee morale. An employee who has come up short for a few months can be redirected, retrained, and helped. Otherwise an employee who has suffered a full year of failure can become incapable of seeing any other way and may just give up and quit.

Three-Year Planning

With a six-month business schedule in place it becomes possible to look at the long-term needs of your company without taking your eye off the day-to-day mechanics of running your business. The mistake many make when taking note of the well-known Japanese preoccupation with the long term, and their willingness to invest to achieve long-term goals, is that effective attention to short-term business requirements is what actually allows many Japanese executives to consider and plan long-term objectives.

In Japan, this long-range thinking usually takes the form of a three-year strategic business plan. Most companies, in their start-up phases, are awash in three-, four-, five-, and even ten-year business plans. However, once capitalized, these plans are sometimes abandoned. In the worst cases, companies become hostages to the marketplace, reacting to events rather than shaping them. In the Western venture capital-driven world, a business plan's main utility often seems to be related to luring money from investors; it is a device used to market the company rather than actually plan its direction.

In most Japanese businesses, however, long-term planning is an ongoing preoccupation. Laid on top of the six-month budgeting cycle usually found in Japanese businesses is a three-year strategic plan, generally updated every year in the December to February time frame. The three-year plan starts off with the budget for the initial six-month period as a foundation and then attempts to predict the opportunities that will become available over the longer term if the company achieves those six-month objectives. In the "out years," the second and third years of the long-term plan, less attention is paid to generating accurate numbers and more attention is given to strategic concerns like enhancing communication about corporate expectations among marketing, product planning, and production divisions.

In addition, the three-year plan provides an opportunity to assess capital investment needs for manufacturing or product development, as well as project probable levels of head counts and the required office space or plant resources. The six-month budget tells employees what they are doing; the three-year plan tells employees and management where the company is heading.

The typical Japanese-style three-year plan, with the six-month budget used as a preface, is not a pie-in-the-sky projection of what the organization might accomplish. Instead, it is intended to be a real-world practical planning vehicle, designed to increase communication within an organization while providing the information managers need to develop realistic, targeted, and coordinated budget plans.

All of this planning and budgeting can be cumbersome at first. When I started at Toshiba, for example, I developed an initial budget for the 1981A six-month period. The next month, I was busy putting together the forecast on the 1981A period while I was also formulating the budget for the 1981B six-month time frame. No sooner had we gotten through that when it was time to do the three-year plan. When that was done, it was time to begin forecasting the 1981B period results as well as to begin to create the 1982 six-month budgets. I've learned, however, that one quickly gets accustomed to this routine, particularly as its useful purposes become apparent.

The value of this process stems from the fact that it puts

managers and employees into a regular cycle of planning and measuring those plans against actual results. New ideas are continually tested and new approaches and experiments are systematically evaluated. Seiko Instruments now updates its three-year plan every January. Part of the review involves comparing the next two years' projections with those formulated in the previous three-year plan, which was crafted 12 months earlier. Then look for changes, pinpoint new opportunities, explains long-term goals, and formulates short-term strategies to accomplish them. The information gleaned from this kind of exercise can be crucial.

Taken together, six-month budgeting, more frequent and regular employee, MBO, bonus, and sales quota evaluations, and a rigorously consistent three-year planning process devoted to enhancing communication and setting company goals allow managers to dump Julius Caesar. Workers and management alike are then able to uncover the more natural rhythms of their business.

The Alchemist's Tool Kit #1
Time and Budget Cycles Checklist

AMERICAN/WESTERN	JAPANESE
Monochronic people:	Polychronic people:
Do one thing at a time	Do many things at once
Have a precise time sense	Have a vague time sense
Are low context and need information	Are high context and already have information
Are committed to a task	Are committed to people and human relationships
One-year budget with emphasis on quarters	Six-month budget with less emphasis on quarters
Yearly MBOs and quota review	Two times per year MBO and quota reviews, and pay out

MANAGEMENT TIPS

- Dump Julius Caesar; establish a six-month planning/budget cycle.

- Do not be ruled by a monochronic sense of time. Keep time—polychronic time—on your side.

- Two times a year budgets and regular once-a-year three-year planning force the planning process to be efficient and regular.

- Use these regular planning and budget cycles to enhance overall employee communications.

- Appreciate and create a sense of variance to budget urgency. Problems fixed in six months are smaller problems.

- Get that second hockey stick. Give employees two major goals, two deadlines per year, to aim at rather than one.

- Employees need more feedback. Give them at least two major performance or MBO evaluations a year. Frequent performance feedback makes work more like the competitive game it is.

- Revise your three-year plan at the same time every year, so it can be compared to the previous three-year plan. The differences are easy to recognize and understand if this is done on a consistent basis.

2

A RACE WITHOUT A FINISH LINE:

Continuous Improvement and How to Make It Work

One of the most important management techniques for management alchemists to understand and adapt is continuous improvement. Known in Japan as *kaizen*, it is the single most important management tool I've encountered. However, because it is culturally based and not easily understood, implementing kaizen with non-Japanese workers can be a very difficult and frustrating process.

Former Chicago Cubs player Vince Law, for example, remembers receiving an unsettling introduction to this age-old Japanese custom of continuous improvement shortly after he signed on as an infielder with Japan's Chunichi Dragons. Law, used to the level of practice in the American major leagues, quickly rebelled at the more fastidious Japanese approach. "We had literally three meetings a day," he complained wearily to an American reporter. "One to go over the scouting report, one to go over the conditions of the field, and then, after the game, the biggest joke of all, a meeting to review everybody's mistakes."

The Japanese ballplayers, according to Law, accepted these constant meetings as routine. But Law, unaccustomed to the principles of kaizen, saw them as negative reinforcement. He simply could not appreciate what appeared to him to be a Japanese fixation with reviewing what had gone wrong, who had made which mistakes, and what could be improved.

The Japanese ballplayers, on the other hand, because of their earliest family, school, and work experiences, regarded these tough kaizen meetings as normal. The talented American infielder, however, was more accustomed to the praise and encouragement common to American-style learning. Law found his experience with Japanese continuous improvement techniques frustrating and, ultimately, counterproductive.

Over the years, I've found that Japanese-style kaizen techniques can be a very effective management tool, but only if they are tempered with appropriate amounts of praise and appreciation. This lesson may take time to assimilate. In fact, at first I had no idea that vastly different preconceptions of the nature of work are involved.

My first clue came shortly after I joined Toshiba as general manager of the U.S. computer division. I noticed that my Japanese managers, who set very, very tough targets, were constantly involved at a shirt-sleeve level with lower-ranking employees. The tough targets, along with constant manager-employee interaction, provided regular opportunities to learn how to improve company performance. Fine. Okay. But before long I noticed that there was something much more than just communication going on.

My Japanese colleagues, managers and employees alike, were, like the Chunichi Dragons, constantly criticizing themselves. They almost seemed to rejoice in their mistakes; at a minimum, they evidenced no fear of admitting errors. To be sure, they did not like or tolerate mistakes for long, but the shame traditionally attached to a mistake in North American and European companies was nowhere to be found.

When I expressed my surprise at this practice, I was often told, mangling an old Western saw, "mistakes are the mother of invention." When Japanese managers and employees make a mistake they quickly admit it. But they do not bother to explain it. Instead, they focus on the countermeasures they plan to take to remedy the problem. The biggest mistake you can make is not to admit you have made a mistake. Once the mistake is admitted, solutions become possible. If the mistake is not acknowledged, the underlying problem can persist indefinitely. As the Japanese are apt to say, "It's never too late to mend."

In addition, by publicly admitting the mistake everybody, not just one individual, can learn from it. For that reason, at Seiko Instruments, USA, the employee mission statement explicitly notes that "we embrace risk taking and tolerate mistakes." What is not tolerated is the failure to admit a mistake or the unwillingness to share those lessons with others. This feature of kaizen—the willingness to use criticism for its most constructive purposes—is the best aspect of the Japanese process of continuous improvement.

However, even more startling than the surfeit of criticism I encountered at Toshiba was the almost total absence of praise or individual employee recognition. This became particularly apparent once Toshiba's U.S. operation began to gain ground. After some initial difficulties, it quickly started hitting and then exceeding sales goals. Swelled with pride, I waited for the plaudits. They never came.

This was especially frustrating. I'd worked very hard to turn things around, yet there were no "attaboys" or "attagirls" for me or my dedicated staff. No pats on the back. No demonstrable appreciation. Instead, there was just more criticism, more analysis of the techniques that led to success, more pressure to do more, sell more, produce greater results. No one said thank you. The constructive criticism, clearly called for when we were failing initially, never let up—even when we were succeeding. It all seemed very pushy to me and, like Vince Law, I began to wonder what kind of thoughtless taskmasters I had come under.

Slowly, however, I realized the constant, unrelenting criticism was totally unrelated to our performance at any one point in time. Instead, I came to understand that kaizen is a constant factor, meaning much more than just "continuous improvement." It is, more accurately, a general Japanese philosophy of life that has enormous consequences in the business world. This philosophy, if modified appropriately, has the potential to become even more effective in business settings outside Japan.

It is necessary to understand that this unspoken system of thought is deeply ingrained in the Japanese mentality, so much so that many who possess it are not consciously aware of its effects on their performance or their views of the abilities of others. At the same time, those who have no exposure to kaizen, mostly non-Japanese, are at risk of omitting an enormously powerful workplace improvement technique from their personal toolbox.

Kaizen is an ancient Japanese concept that is frequently misunderstood to mean "quality control." Masaki Imai's superb book, *Kaizen* (1986), with its emphasis on the minutia of manufacturing, left many with the impression that kaizen is a term that refers strictly to production issues. After reading Imai's book and comparing it to my experiences in the Japanese workplace, I came to appreciate kaizen's decidedly more expansive influence.

While many Western managers are beginning to understand the power of kaizen in improving quality control in the factory, few of them understand how the concept applies to the white-collar work environment. In white-collar fields, management, sales, and the like, the practice of kaizen is also vitally important in Japan, leading to ongoing improvements in virtually all areas of business activity. This concentration may be easier for Japanese workers, since nearly every person's career includes a serious experience in the company factory, often lasting a year or longer. This exposure to the factory makes it easier for Japanese workers to extend factory-oriented kaizen practices into the white-collar parts of their organization.

Kaizen touches every aspect of most Japanese businesses—not just manufacturing, but sales, marketing, and even baseball. However, "quality control"—one of the most frequent mistranslations of kaizen—is a phrase that completely misses the most important nuances of kaizen and obscures its practical importance. In Japan, kaizen is an almost spiritual force. It enables Japanese managers to get more from their people: more quality, more product, more sales, and more employee involvement.

The word "kaizen" can better be defined as a kind of voluntary continuous ("kai") improvement ("zen"), with an emphasis on the voluntary and consensual nature of the process. The kaizen philosophy is a deeply ingrained part of the Japanese culture. Its influence can be seen in Japanese art, for example, where it is not unusual to find artists who devote themselves to the mastery of one narrow discipline, like sculpting birds or bicycles or drawing pond scenes, perfecting their work over a lifetime rather than looking for new challenges. Skilled Japanese calligraphers, those who cultivate bonsai trees, and dedicated martial artists all illustrate the kaizen drive toward achieving perfection.

The kaizen process—and it is most certainly a process rather than a result—is one of the most important management styles I've learned from the Japanese. It explains both the most exasperating aspects of working for the Japanese as well as the astonishing results they so often achieve. I've also learned how to improve the kaizen process for use outside Japan, where unrelenting criticism can and does backfire.

Rather than focus on an event, like keeping quality constant, kaizen forces managers to stay focused on the process, continually improving every facet of it. The ability to concentrate on continuous, small incremental improvement of business processes is a very powerful competitive tool. This focus on constantly improving the process of business activities provides managers with their single most effective commercial advantage. It provides the motivation, incentive, and structure for workers to team up with each other to achieve common objectives.

Success as the Mother of Failure

That the word "kaizen" is often misunderstood in the West to mean "quality control" rather than "voluntary continuous improvement" demonstrates a dangerous mind-set. Such a misunderstanding implies that quality, once achieved, need only be controlled, that is, kept constant, in order to assure customer satisfaction. Japanese executives, on the other hand, maintain that "success is the mother of failure."

The results of the static quality control dogma are apparent. *Consumer Reports* magazine, for instance, publishes a list of used cars by year of vintage, rating them on demonstrated attributes like quality, ease of repair, and reliability. While American cars, for example, occasionally score high on the list for a particular year, until recently it was hard to find an American car commended for its quality two years in a row, let alone three or four. Japanese cars, on the other hand, rarely fall off the good list once they make their first appearance. Thanks to the competitive pressures of the global marketplace, this situation is starting to change. American automakers have finally realized they must adapt and apply

Japanese kaizen techniques to their factories and show-rooms. At places like the Nummi plant in California and the GM Saturn facility in Tennessee, this new American-style kaizen is already at work, yielding tangible results.

As the Japanese saying regarding the motherhood of failure conveys, hubris is the enemy of kaizen's voluntary continuous improvement. The worst thing that can happen to companies is meeting goals or attaining success. The temptation to rest on one's laurels is too great. It can lead to debilitating setbacks. By putting the emphasis on constantly improving the process no matter what the result, kaizen serves to neutralize hubris.

By emphasizing concern with the work process as much as with the result, a kaizen approach can help managers be better problem-solvers when things go wrong and better opportunists at other times. It is possible to find areas for improvement in places many results-oriented managers would not spend five minutes thinking about. When you go into a Japanese company, for example, you find charts and graphs posted all over the place, measuring every business, manufacturing, sales, and management activity. Every department seems to have its own set of charts and graphs, which are updated regularly and which serve as barometers of the group's performance. In most cases, these charts are created by the workers and employees themselves, not by some corporate communication department.

At Seiko Instruments, USA, I worked hard to make sure our people realized that these charts represent *group* goals and targets. Taking the spotlight off the individual and putting it on the group makes it easier for people to feel comfortable about admitting mistakes at every step and reporting them to management right away. Managers are then able to continuously improve the total work process by constantly scrutinizing their operations. Once the process is improved, the results take care of themselves.

Some managers are famous for instructions like, "I don't care how you do it, just get it done." Managers using kaizen techniques would never say that; instead, they want to know exactly how it was done, whether it can be done better, and whether other ways have been tried. Once a task is finished, the questions keep coming. The focus shifts from what was achieved to how it was achieved, how it can be done better and faster next time.

Oddly enough, in Japan, where it is second-nature, the kaizen approach is sometimes too powerful. The attitude that everything can be continuously improved sometimes leaves Japanese managers unwilling to take more drastic steps, such as closing down a clearly losing operation when doing so is really necessary. Outside Japan, where such concerns are not a factor, this management technique can be modified and improved to yield some very beneficial results.

Adding Positive Feedback

In the kaizen culture, 100% of everyone's energy goes into improving the process. There is constant albeit constructive criticism. Even in Japan, where kaizen is understood on a cultural level, such criticism can be disheartening. However, most Japanese I've come across would be worried if they were *not* criticized by their bosses; they would be concerned that their work is so inferior that even the boss thinks it cannot be improved. Remarkably, most Japanese workers I've encountered do seem to regard constructive criticism as a form of positive feedback from their bosses. At least, they've told me, they know they are not being ignored or given up on.

Outside Japan, however, it is crucial to intersperse constructive criticism with sincere praise. For example, my staff and I were simply stunned at Toshiba to receive so little praise for helping build a business from zero to $350 million dollars-plus a year in sales in less than a decade. At a certain point, without some positive feedback, employees feel so unappreciated that their performance is affected. The Japanese are certainly not immune from this human response even if they do seem to be able to tolerate a higher level of unremitting criticism. However, most organizational behavior experts seem to agree that positive feedback, missing in many traditional Japanese organizations, is an essential part of managing productivity growth and improvement.

Western managers have an opportunity to improve productivity gained through the use of kaizen techniques by adding praise to the criticism. Due to cultural factors, it will be a long time before the average Japanese manager feels comfortable praising individual workers. For that reason, Western managers can derive even greater benefits from kaizen than are now seen in many Japanese organizations. By tempering criticism with some Western-style praise and appreciation, managers can create an improved form of kaizen, one that welcomes constant criticism and improvement within a nonthreatening framework.

This will require some subtle changes in orientation. For example, typical Japanese employees, according to Japanese businessman Aki Tsurakame, "know the company exists for them and they want it to continue." This helps reinforce the kaizen focus on the work process, says Tsurakame, because employees "want to improve themselves and their company."

Because they fail to understand Japanese-style kaizen, many workers tend to take criticism far too personally. Implicit in the criticism, employees often feel, is the assumption that they did not do their best, that the boss could have or would have done better. Employees generally feel they are being blamed if even one valid critical observation can be made.

In the kaizen context, however, the same criticism can take on a more welcome tone. If it is made clear to all con-

31

cerned that the goal of voluntary continuous improvement can never be totally attained, and if everyone knows and accepts this fact, it comes as no disgrace when areas of potential improvement are pointed out.

If combined with praise and genuine appreciation, this new form of the kaizen process takes the onus off the individual and puts it where it belongs: on the process, on the total group performance over the long term.

For example, I have a friend who is responsible for two factories—one in Japan and the other in the United States. Both factories produce the same product. The facilities are roughly equal in every way except one: the Japanese factory consistently outperforms the American one. What accounts for the difference? kaizen. My friend explains: "Both factories set the same target and they both may hit it. But when the Japanese hit it they keep going whereas the Americans tend to stop and rest on their laurels before pursuing the next goal." I'm currently trying to convince my friend that a modified kaizen strategy could help the American factory outperform the Japanese factory.

The spirit required for such a change was apparent in the comments of the captain of Japan's 1964 Olympic women's volleyball team, which galvanized Japan with an unexpected gold medal in the Tokyo games. Explaining the team's success, the victorious captain remarked: "If we stop when we achieve something, then we will only half succeed. Instead, we look at it as a platform to achieve more. Then, when we achieve some more, that is a platform to achieve even more." The other volleyball players at the Olympics were undoubtedly unaware that kaizen played such an important role in their defeat.

Much like Aesop's fable of the race between the tortoise and the hare, many managers, like the hare, are driven by events. They are impatient and want to get ahead. And once there, they feel they have earned the right to take a nap. Aesop's tortoise, on the other hand, seemed to instinctively understand kaizen, that winning requires a constant and steady effort over time.

This lesson seems lost on many Westerners. Too often, leading businesses in the West have been content to take a single step, like inventing the VCR, from zero to one, while the Japanese, who were unwilling or unable to take that first step, are ready to make the more profitable run from one to infinity, constantly improving the product, commercializing it, and building market share. In between these two poles, managers can find ways to achieve more, by welcoming innovation and continuously striving for perfection with the goal of achieving excellence. Adding positive feedback to kaizen-style criticism, and making certain such criticism is routine and expected, provides managers with a powerful ongoing motivational tool.

The long-term striving for perfection implicit in the kaizen style also reduces the importance of short-term excuses—even those based on time pressures or deadlines. When a deadline is offered to excuse some deficit, an effective manager motivated by the kaizen spirit should remain nonplussed. If appropriate, she might even ask why a deadline was established or tolerated if it interfered with perfection. A deadline, even a hard and fast one set by some external force, never means the job is finished. Deadlines are merely points at which you measure progress; they are not the end of the process. The process, imbued with a constant appreciation of kaizen, never ends. Business conducted in this fashion is a race without a finish line.

Real Work versus Nonreal Work

Westerners tend to overlook the importance of work process concerns, preferring to focus almost entirely on the results. Some of my non-Japanese colleagues have even referred to process issues as "nonreal" work, compared with the real work of selling or manufacturing.

For example, I take part in a business roundtable group, the Southern California Technology Execution Network (SOCALTEN) managers and executives meet regularly to share workplace improvement strategies aimed at getting people to focus on process issues. We've had many discussions about these concerns, and new process-oriented approaches are being implemented at many of these companies. But the transition has not been easy.

In general, Westerners have a deep-seated and strong bias against taking the time required to carefully measure progress and make process improvements when necessary. Undoubtedly, cultural factors rooted in early childhood education and workplace experiences account for much of this difference. While I'm not an anthropologist, there is some evidence that these differences go quite deep.

At Seiko Instruments, USA, for example, we retained a team of experienced consultants to help our American employees develop a continuous improvement kaizen program, which became the model for the modified kaizen approach currently in use. Early on, the consultants confirmed what I had long suspected: their biggest hurdle was overcoming our Western prejudice against so-called nonreal work. The consultants told me that my employees must be made explicitly aware of the links between nonreal work, such as bringing costs down, and the real work of the company. This linkage is apparent to most Japanese workers, but needs to be emphasized more directly outside Japan.

This type of kaizen-oriented nonreal work should not be confused with the nonwork performed by many members of the typical corporate or government bureaucracy, who often generate plenty of unimportant tasks aimed primarily at justifying their jobs. The big difference is that these paperwork managers are usually too remote from their workforce or too out-of-touch with the product or service provided to offer any real help. In Japan, kaizen is practiced at every step by the line managers themselves. They focus on the nonreal work of improving their methods and practices, but do not waste time with unimportant work that removes them from the front lines of their businesses.

For the successful Japanese manager, so-called nonreal work is every bit as important as the rest. The common Shinto/Buddhist religious background shared by 98% of the Japanese, which emphasizes that all humanity is constantly seeking an ever-elusive state of perfection, helps predispose the Japanese toward a process of constant incremental improvements. It is, however, certainly possible for Westerners to emulate this practice without sacrificing identities or beliefs.

The best way a manager can achieve this objective is to first understand and convey to employees the western cultural resistance to nonreal work. Linking some nonreal work activities, such as producing an improvement that leads to faster responses to customer inquiries, to real-world rewards like improved customer retention and increased sales and profits, is a good way to demonstrate the importance of nonreal work. Pointing out, for example, that decreased invoice error rates, improved on-time shipments, or reduced stock shortages lead to more job opportunities, pay raises, bonuses, and career advancement opportunities is another useful technique.

Although it may seem obvious, it is important to explicitly draw this link between nonreal work and real results, like job security and professional growth. The point is that the process by which work gets done, and the striving for continuous improvement of that process, is even more important than the eventual result, because it is the process which creates that result. Worry about the process and the result should take care of itself; worrying only about the result may mean that chances to improve the process will be missed.

The Japanese concept of *kata*, literally meaning "the way," is also instructive. Kata holds there is a proper way to do everything. There is a perfect way to pour tea, for example. The elaborate tea ceremonies, still commonplace in Japan, are yet another manifestation of the innate Japanese drive toward perfection. As Japanese management guru Masaru Chioio puts it, the Japanese "are perfectionists. They notice the slightest problem or anything that attracts their attention and they cannot rest until after it is eliminated."

In his book, *The Kata Factor*, Boyd DeMente points out that, for centuries, the Japanese were conditioned to get their pleasure from conforming to kata and doing things in a precise, proscribed manner. Thus, it is not surprising that when Japanese employees are evaluated by their superiors, the focus is always on attitude first, effort second, and results third. The question is not so much what the employee has done as it is whether the employee is trying hard and doing it in the right way.

By understanding the cultural and religious background that spawned kaizen we can uncover what has made the process of voluntary continuous improvement "second-nature" to the Japanese. It is then possible to identify the cultural predispositions that must be overcome in order to move yourself, and your organization, into an invigorating kaizen mode of thought.

In the end, the kaizen approach provides a wonderful opportunity to make widespread voluntary continuous improvements. This will build your company, or your division, work group, or department, into a place where personal growth is enabled, encouraged, and rewarded.

This is a "baby step" approach to management. Recently, for example, ETAK, the company I now lead, got bogged down in lengthy negotiations with the U.S. government over a joint venture research and development project. Our people were simply paralyzed by the need they felt to articulate their shared final vision for this project. However, they could not really get started in earnest because they could not figure out how it would end. Take "baby steps" I told them, explaining the kaizen mentality. They quickly divided the work into digestible portions. One group went to work figuring out reasonable first steps while another group sketched out a variety of possible long-term options. The logjam was broken because they focused on moving one log at a time, not the whole forest.

This is a difficult and subtle but critically important change in orientation. And it does not depend on changing the educational or financial system to make it happen. As a manager, you are the key. And in business, it is attention to building a successful kaizen culture that, over the long term, will separate the winners from the losers.

Plan—Do—See

One of the easiest and most practical tools with which to build this Western kaizen culture is through the use of the simple plan—do—see routine that I first encountered at Toshiba.

One of the first promotional campaigns I crafted for Toshiba involved placing demo laptop computers in retail outlets. The idea, a mainstay of the computer business, is very simple: Give away products at or near cost to dealers in exchange for their promise that the units will be used to bolster sales. So just add up the number of retail outlets and ship them all a demo unit with operating instructions, right? Wrong.

Using the plan—do—see approach requires that goals for our demo program, and for the process itself, be set before we initiated it, so that we could measure the success of the campaign as it went along.

How many more units will you sell because of the demo program? How will you make sure that the dealers don't just sell the demo unit at full retail price? When will you be able to see a difference in the sales numbers? What will be the difference, in terms of sales per store, between a retail outlet with a demo unit and one without a demo unit? What is the shelf-life of a demo unit? What price will dealers pay for a demo unit? The questions are endless. Process-oriented managers establish targets that can serve as benchmarks. Then, if we don't hit the target for each area, they ask themselves what they can do next time to improve results.

These are the practical mechanics of Plan—Do—See. A thorough analysis is always the first step. That you cannot accurately project how many sales will result from a demo placement program matters little. What matters is that targets, for both sales and for the actual demo process itself, be established.

• Plan: Understand and rank alternatives, select a course of action, and set targets for achievement.
• Do: Implement the chosen course of action.
• See: Measure the performance and the progress against the process targets or goals that have been set.

This cycle then repeats itself—part of the ongoing kaizen process. The step missed by many western managers, the kaizen step in the process, is the "see" step, arguably the most important of the three. The Japanese offer a consistent criticism on this point: "You westerners love to plan things. You're okay at doing them, but you don't have the patience for the seeing part. You just want to always go on to the next project."

By seeing we learn, so that on the next round of problem-solving or opportunity analysis we benefit from our experience and become better orchestrators of the programs and projects for which we are responsible. Regardless of your position in a company, you can use plan—do—see to enhance your performance and gain ultimate job satisfaction. But to see you must know what you are looking for.

Seeing, kaizen-style, is much more than noting whether you have hit your targets. At Toshiba it meant, among other things, ghost or mystery shopping, sending our people into retail outlets to see how well the demo units are being used. We want to know if the sales clerks need more training. We want to know if there are particular software programs that work better in the demo setting. We want to know if it matters where in the store a demo unit is positioned. We want to know if a point-of-sale display around the demo unit increases sales. In addition to measuring the actual sales we produce, we're also just as interested in learning everything we can about the processes used to garner those sales.

Simply put, Toshiba wanted to quantify everything regarding expectations for the sales demo program, measuring results against forecasts. It is not simply a matter of shipping out the newest demo units and counting the orders as they roll in. That is not seeing.

Instead, the focus is on the whole process, how the demo unit process works, and how the principles of kaizen will make it more effective. Subjecting activities to constant criticism and carefully focusing on the process and not just the result, creates a culture in which something is being improved every day.

Routinely encourage my staff to use the plan—do—see technique as often as possible. Frequently, I'll say, "let's do a 'see' on the project we've just completed." The key to making this technique work is to establish targets when you formulate any given plan. Even in the absence of such targets, it is still valuable to go through the rigor of doing a see. Making these explicit see steps a routine part of your workplace activities is an excellent way to get employees to regard regular doses of criticism as a normal and commonplace business activity.

Suggestion Systems

Another effective way to create a Western form of kaizen in your company is through an effective suggestion system. Little more than a stage prop in many companies, the employee suggestion system is a centerpiece of effective people management at the most successful Japanese companies. Hiroki Kato estimates that fully 90% of new ideas in Japanese auto companies come "from the bottom up," not from the R&D or design departments.

The kaizen philosophy is partly responsible for this—working in both directions on the Japanese organizational chart. The kaizen spirit helps generate the effective teamwork required in modern business environments and provides the philosophical underpinning of the Japanese reliance on employee suggestion systems.

Just as the Japanese boss feels a responsibility to offer constructive criticism to employees, Japanese employees, imbued with kaizen, likewise feel it their duty to improve their companies whenever possible.

In Japan, the suggestion system is usually a group-oriented activity. The typical Japanese workgroup, the *ka*, which consists of 10 to 15 people, is frequently broken down into an even smaller group, the *shogroup*, which means "small group." Shogroups form what the president of Kyocera once called the "amoeba" of a Japanese company.

These shogroups are constantly coming up with suggestions on how to improve the processes within their domain of responsibility. The suggestions from each shogroup are measured weekly, and there is enormous pressure to match or exceed the number of suggestions being made by other shogroups in the company. At Seiko Instruments, USA, we've started to form these Japanese-style small workgroups, but, for the most part, the employee suggestion system is still primarily aimed at individuals. We try to avoid the turmoil that sometimes takes place when one small workgroup is pitted against another while making use of the advantages a highly visible employee suggestion system provides.

A friend of mine, who works for a Japanese car company in the United States, illustrated this point, complaining that the competition among shogroups, even in the United States, is tough. Sometimes she was forced to work harder and put in extra hours to maintain a competitive level of workplace suggestions for her group. When I asked her, however, if she felt this practice had helped her company and made her feel like a more important part of the team, her response was a quick affirmation, though the pressure was clearly wearing her down.

The very fact that Japanese companies respect and empower these small groups of workers through quality circles, zero defect groups, and shogroups does, however, demonstrate that management really cares about what these people think. Often, I've heard workers refer to their employment in a very dispirited way; "it's only a job," they say. The same people, if given respect and power, are attracted to the idea that they can have a real influence on their company. "Only a job" becomes "*my* job," and "the company" becomes "*my* company."

Shogroups are more highly empowered than any one individual within the average Japanese company. Working together, these small teams accomplish far more than any single worker ever could. As a rule, the department, or *ka*, made up of several shogroups, is responsible for achieving the group's sales and profit targets while the shogroups within the department have the ongoing responsibility for making and suggesting process improvements for their group. The shogroups regularly report their progress, and individual shogroup members, no matter how young, take turns detailing their group's suggestions to the other shogroups.

When it comes to implementing an employee suggestion system, Japanese managers have an advantage because Japanese workers are convinced that improvements they suggest, if implemented, will better their own lives. In Japan, participating in a suggestion system is seen as far more than doing a favor for the company. The employees are doing themselves and their colleagues a favor. They know it, they feel it—and they do it.

When, for example, the Aspen Institute asked who would benefit from improvements employees might make in their companies, 93% of Japanese respondents said that they, themselves, would benefit. Only 9% of U.S. workers surveyed gave that answer. This is a stunning difference: The degree to which workers identify their own personal progress with the progress of their company accounts for a vast difference in the effort, dedication, and productivity of employees. The higher level of job security typically enjoyed by most Japanese workers only partially accounts for this dramatic difference. In fact, it can be argued that job security in Japan is as much a result of these other factors, like successful suggestion systems, as it is a cause.

Given their shogroup orientation, Japanese-style employee suggestion systems differ markedly from the usual Western versions. At Seiko Instruments USA, for example, two senior U.S. managers were asked to develop a suggestion box system for employees. The program they proposed was typically American. It was designed to elicit blockbuster ideas. It established financial rewards only for those suggestions that resulted in savings in excess of $2,000 per year. The entire focus was on finding spectacular one-shot, dramatic breakthroughs. IBM, in a similar fashion, provides a $150,000 prize for each year's top money-saving idea.

Experience with Japanese-style suggestion systems taught me this approach was all wrong. While it was not feasible to establish the Japanese shogroup suggestion system, I did send my managers back to the drawing board and instructed them to come up with a system that encouraged broader participation. I was more interested in soliciting ideas that would generate the small incremental improvements that cumulatively mean so much to a business.

Managers should always be on the lookout for these small, do-able incremental improvements which, in turn, lead to the creation of effective teams. If only super efforts are counted as important, workers are apt to stop making more routine contributions to their organizations.

The Japan Human Relations Association recently illustrated the effects of this different approach. A survey they conducted compares employee suggestion systems in Japan and the United States. U.S. companies, the survey demonstrated, routinely look for the home run suggestion, the major breakthrough, the one-time dramatic event. Japanese managers, on the other hand, practice kaizen by encouraging constant incremental process improvements. They solicit and reward all suggestions, home runs as well as singles; even times at bat are rewarded. The comparison is startling. By generating more employee involvement, more ideas, and more suggestions, Japanese managers get more productivity from and for their people.

The study also reveals the effects of poorly structured suggestion systems. If employees feel that management only values the big ideas, they will be more reluctant, even embarrassed, to make suggestions that will result in only minor improvements.

Japan		*United States*
1,936,738	# of potential participants	9,194,762
47,926,020	# of suggestions	1,246,749
24.7	# of suggestions per person	0.14
$3.26	prize money per proposal	$416
$231,770	economic benefit produced per each 100 potential participants	$19,995

Clearly, a multitude of minor suggestions means much more to the bottom line than a handful of blockbuster ideas. Seiko Instrument, USA, awards a helium-filled pink balloon to each worker who submitted a suggestion the previous week. Each Tuesday, pink balloons float above the desks of workers. While this may seem a little saccharin to more jaded workers, it is vital to find means to acknowledge the receipt of each suggestion quickly, within days, as a way of constantly reinforcing the suggestion program. Instead of balloons, for example, you can award points that can be exchanged for products made by the company, tickets to sporting events, or some other tangible but inexpensive reward.

Although it may take time to determine if it makes sense to actually implement any given suggestion, it is essential that employees be recognized immediately for making the effort. At Seiko Instruments, USA, once a suggestion is implemented, the employee receives either $10 for a good idea or $20 for a great idea. Then, each month, there is a blind drawing out of a hat filled with the names of all those who submitted suggestions in the prior period with a $250 prize. All employees who make a suggestion, even a minor one, are eligible to win the biggest award. Small ideas are important, and employees are constantly reminded of this fact.

The suggestion system serves to keep the profile of the program high as well as provide tangible rewards to those who participate in it. While the rewards are mostly symbolic, the egalitarian nature of the effort produces the widest possible participation. The emphasis, part of the kaizen approach, is always on getting the greatest number of people to take part in the suggestion system as a regular part of their work routine.

I've seen suggestion systems at work in nearly every successful company I have ever visited. At these companies there are usually posters in the lunchroom to remind employees of the program and announcements are made, often on a weekly basis, noting which department has submitted the most suggestions. Signs are put up honoring recent participants, and workers are continually reminded of the program and invited to offer their ideas. Doing so is a matter of departmental pride.

According to the *Los Angeles Times,* many U.S. businesses have ample room to do a better job in this regard. "In a nation [the United States] of 200,000 companies that employ 50 or more people," the *Times* reports, "only about 6,000 firms are believed to operate suggestion systems." About 1,000 of these U.S. companies belong to the National Association of Suggestion Systems, which calculates that its member organizations saved $2.3 billion by implementing employee suggestions. And that astonishing performance came with only a tiny fraction of U.S. industry participating.

In Japan, the Honda Motor Company now awards free cars to those making major money-saving suggestions. However, that is still the exception. More often, employees are rewarded with small token gifts like a coffee mug, a balloon, some special recognition, or a brass nameplate, given for each suggestion—whether implemented or not. This type of reward system keeps the visibility of the program high within the company.

Seiko Instruments is working hard at increasing the visibility and status of those who investigate the feasibility of implementing individual suggestions. In the past, this has been a time-consuming and thankless task, usually performed by top management. However, we discovered that by creating a small evaluation team composed of representatives from each discipline and managerial level in the company we were able to keep our suggestion program vibrant. Suggestion system programs often die out after a while, so by periodically rotating in a new employee-led evaluation team, and publicizing their activities in the company newsletter we maintain the momentum of our program. At Seiko Instruments, USA, we rotated the membership of the suggestion system evaluation committee every six months to get as many people participating in the program as possible and to make room for fresh perspectives. Sometimes, a suggestion rejected by one evaluation committee might be found valuable by a different committee, composed of different members, at a different time.

While we kept our focus on getting individuals to participate, we moved closer to the shogroup model by establishing a target for the number of suggestions a department is expected to generate. In order to prime the system and jumpstart initial participation, these targets now appear in the job descriptions and bonus objectives of department managers. The goal is to get one suggestion per employee every six months. As humble as this sounds, it is still way above the American average. At some leading companies, like Motorola, the target is higher—around one suggestion per employee each quarter, or even one per month. In Asia, Motorola's employees often put in one suggestion per week! Establishing a vibrant suggestion system helps create a climate of continual change and improvement.

In larger Japanese companies, entire departments are sometimes rewarded with a three-day vacation retreat in return for the most suggestions. Only rarely, however, are individuals singled out in Japan, as the focus is nearly always placed on total group performance. However, it is possible to find a middle ground between Western and Japanese approaches, one that rewards individual accomplishments within the framework of a harmonious group. Creating a company culture in which everyone's ideas are solicited, evaluated, and rewarded is an excellent way to get everyone living and breathing the kaizen spirit.

The Alchemist's Tool Kit #2
Continuous Improvement Checklist

AMERICAN/WESTERN	JAPANESE
Task	Process
Real work	Nonreal work
Plan—Do	Plan—Do—See
9% of Americans believe they will personally benefit from company improvement	93% of Japanese believe they will personally benefit from company improvement

Suggestion Systems
  Home runs
  Individual rewards
	Suggestion Systems
	  Singles
	  Group rewards

MANAGEMENT TIPS

- The biggest mistake you can make is not admitting when you make a mistake. Otherwise, you cannot learn from it until it negatively affects the whole organization.

- Include the encouragement of risk-taking and tolerating mistakes in your company employees mission statement.

- Build an environment that encourages incremental improvements derived from every conceivable source.

- The "baby step" philosophy leads to small incremental phased solutions.

- Improve Japanese kaizen techniques by interposing constant criticism with some Western-style praise.

- Focus on improving the process; the result will take care of itself.

- Understand the Western cultural bias for real work over nonreal work. Draw a clear linkage between continuous improvement and cost savings and employee benefit.

- Post charts and graphs for all improvement programs. Have workers prepare these charts themselves.

- Use the plan—do—see cycle consistently. Measure progress of the program processes as well as task results. Do not neglect the see step.

- Implement a broad-based employee suggestion system. Solicit both ideas and constructive criticism. Give immediate recognition to all suggesters with pink balloon or other tokens of recognition. Rewards should be symbolic and visible. Continually reinforce the program with some larger, but egalitarian, recognition.

- Remember that success is the mother of failure.

3

REAL WORK:

Why the Art of the Relationship Comes before the Art of the Deal

Many Westerners see their "real work" as the aspects of their jobs that can be quantified: budgets met, accounts established, the number of projects completed. Most everything else, establishing relationships with customers and colleagues, for example, is "nonreal"—nice to do but not counting for much when it comes to goals and evaluations. Management alchemists, however, need to see things differently. As I show in this chapter, bigger and better deals will result if more time and attention are paid to "nonreal" work. Here's a significant opportunity to capture the essence of the way business is done in another culture and blend it into our own.

The importance of relationships became apparent when I interviewed for my position at Toshiba America, Inc. The first thing the company president, Mr. Kobayashi, said to me was, "This is the third time we have met." It was not a passing remark. For him, there was great significance in the fact that we had already shared some prior experiences. A year earlier, in my capacity as a consultant for International Data Corporation, I had presented Mr. Kobayashi and his colleagues at Toshiba with a special report on the computer industry. Some months later, I invited my new contacts at Toshiba to attend a Picasso exhibit in New York, which they very much enjoyed. Although those prior interactions were of a fleeting nature, for Mr. Kobayashi they were a foothold. All our subsequent discussions built on the fact that we had already established some kind of relationship as a result of those brief encounters.

As my job interview unfolded, Mr. Kobayashi asked most of the questions I had anticipated. We covered the technical side of the business. Product histories and management philosophies were discussed. However, I was surprised that fully 50% of the interview was spent exploring topics that had nothing at all to do with the computer business or Toshiba. Mr. Kobayashi was interested, sincerely interested in my hobbies, my family, and my favorite sports and leisure activities. His obvious enthusiasm for learning these details, which he carefully noted, was central to the interviewing process.

I left our meeting feeling that Mr. Kobayashi appreciated me as a person; and I decided right then and there that if the terms offered were even close to what I sought I wanted to be a member of the Toshiba team. I had not made a deal with Mr. Kobayashi, nor had he with me. Instead, Mr. Kobayashi and I had successfully commenced the building of a strong, mutually beneficial relationship.

A similar story has been told and retold by Japanese businesspeople for years: A Westerner seeking to initiate a business deal calls or writes the prospective partner and makes his pitch. The same day, a Japanese businessman calls the same prospective partner, but does not mention his proposal and does not make his pitch. His request is different: "Would you like to play golf sometime?" The Japanese businessman usually wants to build a personal relationship first while the Westerner usually wants to make a deal first. Guess which approach is more effective over time? And guess which deals are more likely to fall apart under pressure?

It is not a simple matter of "hard-selling" Westerner versus "soft-selling" Japanese. The Japanese are quite sincere. They want much more than a deal or a sale. They want a customer not just for today, but for life. They want a long-term relationship, not a short-term deal.

To be sure, sometimes the Japanese go overboard in this regard. I've even heard of Japanese salespersons visiting each of their customers every day, just to say "hello." This approach does make it emotionally difficult for the customer to switch suppliers. However, practices like this contribute to Japan's lagging overall worker productivity rates, including the notoriously inefficient product distribution system.

In fact, Japan's product distribution system is so inefficient it serves as a drag on the overall Japanese economy. According to a McKinsey Global Institute 1992 study, while Japan has a comfortable productivity edge in manufacturing such key products as electronics and autos, it lags far behind the United States in overall worker productivity. In the retail sector the difference is particularly large, with the United States enjoying a 2-1 productivity edge over Japan. Additionally, as compared with U.S. companies, Japanese industry requires more people to produce the same number of goods in a wide range of market sectors, including chemicals, petroleum, textiles and apparels, rubber and plastics, and food products. These figures demonstrate that there is sometimes a productivity price to be paid if honoring an extended network of human relationships comes at the expense of economic efficiency. It is an open question whether Japanese industry can continue to tolerate such practices; it does seem likely that market pressures will force Japanese industry more toward the U.S. model. However, as one Japanese scholar points out, Japan's product distribution system is not intended to be efficient in the strict sense. "It's really Japan's welfare system," noted Japanese economist and businessman Aki Tsurakame explains.

Telemarketing, a sometimes annoying but booming sales technique in the United States, is still not widespread in Japan. Buying products over the phone from a stranger remains an uncomfortable and unusual experience for most Japanese. Generally speaking, it is just not done. When it is practiced, the Japanese telemarketer is usually just an order taker—leaving the maintenance of the customer/vendor relationship in the hands of individual salesforce "foot soldiers." Clearly, the full-blown emphasis on relationship-building can and occasionally does go too far.

However, the focus on building relationships is an aspect of Japanese culture that also offers some profoundly powerful advantages. And, unlike the Japanese, most American managers seem to be in no danger of being too familiar with their employees, customers, vendors, or business partners. Both sides would do well to move their practices more to the center of the relationship-building spectrum.

Workers typically respond very well when strong interpersonal relationships are nurtured at work. For example, when you ask a Japanese whom he or she works for, you will receive a unique answer: "I belong to Toshiba" or "I belong to Sony." This sense of belonging illustrates the importance the Japanese place on relationships as opposed to situations.

Of course, given the American corporate propensity for layoffs and alienation of workers, is often impractical to expect the same degree of loyalty from American employees. That kind of loyalty has to be earned. However, managers can move their employees farther along the loyalty continuum by placing the emphasis on relationships rather than transactions. The art of the deal is in the relationship.

Additionally, the old adage is very true: The best customer is the one you already have. That customer, if satisfied, brings you more business and more customers. The surest way to grow a business is to nurture the growth of your customers' business. This philosophy is the underpinning for the complex web of human relationships within and among Japanese businesses. What seems to many Westerners like a cobweb designed primarily to hamstring foreign businesses operating in the Japanese domestic market is seen by the Japanese in a more benign light; to them, it is a finely honed network of interdependent and time-tested relationships that deserve protection from outside forces. Excluding foreigners from their market is not so much the reason or rationale for this pattern of interactions. More accurately, it is the result.

It is not that foreigners cannot penetrate the cobweb as, clearly, numerous foreign businesses have succeeded in Japan; instead, too often, foreigners seem totally unaware that such a network exists. Frustrated, they often spend a lot of their time running around Japan yelling "foul." What the typical "Lone Ranger"-style of businessperson needs to know is that only teams can compete with other teams. Westerners too often approach business like an individual sport. The Japanese, on the other hand, know that business is a team sport. And to win, everyone—suppliers, employees, customers, and vendors—must feel they are an important part of the team.

Japanese managers have told me they see each of their company's interactions with outside suppliers, whether they sell stationery or silicon chips, as an opportunity to form a meaningful strategic alliance. These alliances allow different companies to combine their efforts over a long period of time to achieve common objectives.

The virtual coalition of interests that comprise a successful Japanese team constitutes what has often been called the

Japanese "group ego." I've seen it at work many times. Employees who possess this group ego derive genuine pleasure out of the group's accomplishments. The solidarity of the Japanese work group creates a platform from which effective competition can be staged. Good managers need to ask themselves not only if their product is better than what the competition offers. They also need to ask themselves if their team is as good, as tight, and as group-oriented as it can be.

To illustrate the point: A Japanese friend who runs a Fujitsu group subsidiary in the United States tells me he is often aghast at the conduct of many Americans he meets. They are ignorant, he tells me, of the need to create harmonious teams. "They come in here and the only thing they care about is price," he says, totally amazed that a price differential of a few pennies per hundred dollars is enough for many Westerners to take their business elsewhere. "What they don't realize is all the other things we can do for them if they become one of our customers," he says, most earnestly.

In the end, it is those "other things," like advance word of new product design improvements, a willingness to custom engineer a particular product, ironclad quality guarantees, or specialized delivery terms, which can help a business thrive.

The enormous time investment the typical Japanese businessperson makes to develop and build relationships puts Japanese and Americans at extreme ends of the spectrum, with the rest of the world somewhere in between. To be sure, many corporations have recently begun paying some attention to concepts like customer service. Sadly, however, the effort remains mostly on the lip-service level. Adding a couple of phone lines to handle complaints or asking a salesperson to give more attention to customers fails to come to grips with the reality of the West's largely deal-oriented business culture.

Many of the small businesses that have thrived recently, despite widespread recessionary pressures and the global downsizing of the Fortune 500, are those enterprises that most closely follow the Japanese model of human relationships. Most successful entrepreneurs do not need to be convinced of the importance of building long-term relationships with their customers. That this lesson still eludes the corporate elite is another reflection of the distance too many managers have from their markets, their people, and their products.

My experience in global business has convinced me that most, if not all, cultures place a much greater premium on relationship-building in business than do United States managers and executives. This observation was confirmed recently by *Forbes* magazine, which published a study of the amount of GNP consumed by lawsuits around the world. In the United States, fully 2.5% of GNP is consumed by litigation costs, a figure more than five times higher than that in Japan, the United Kingdom, or Germany. While there may be no direct correlation between relationship-building and lawsuits, there is at least a strong indirect relationship. In America, when a deal goes sour it is time to call in the lawyers and sue. In Japan, when a deal goes sour the relationship, because it has been carefully cultivated, usually survives and the individuals involved are apt to look for other ways to meet their common business objectives.

Relationship-building can be very difficult for Americans. For example, a friend of mine, an account supervisor at the N. W. Ayer advertising agency, spent a lot of time working with executives at Toshiba. Exemplifying the typical Western, and particularly American, reticence, he once told me, "Gee, I understand we're supposed to spend time on relationships, but it seems so phony." The inability to just let go of the pressures of the moment and simply allow a business relationship to develop over time too often characterizes the

Western approach. The revealing comment about the "phoniness" of the exercise would be lost on most Japanese. To them, it is not phony; it is natural and essential. At Seiko Instruments, USA, I always encouraged our employees to attend supplier open houses and join industry associations. These events are often seen as a fun departure from the normal course of business. Of course, the more fun employees have with suppliers and colleagues the better.

As Toshiba's president Joichi Aoi told a reporter from *Financial World* magazine not long ago: "This may sound a bit strange, but I believe we are running a business well if the manager is happy. So if [our manager] is happy, then his business is going well." Of course, there is no way to know if a manager is happy unless there is a strong relationship between the manager and his or her boss. When, for example, I asked one of Seiko Instruments' top managers, Mr. R. Takagi, how I could develop strong ties with Seiko Instruments board members, his response had everything to do with social relationships and nothing at all to do with business. "Play golf with us," he said, "drink with us and go to the *onsen* [hot springs] with us." At the onsen, Mr. Takagi explained, his naked Japanese colleagues get "belly to belly" with each other, which helps deepen their relationships beyond the superficial stage.

To outsiders, it sometimes seems Japanese are willing to accept higher prices from their Japanese suppliers than they will from foreign suppliers. This reality often offends and mystifies Westerners and is a source of much of the trade friction between Japan and the West. However, it is only part of the story. The other part, the more important part, is that when Japanese do occasionally tolerate higher prices from their Japanese suppliers it is often because they are protecting a relationship that may go back generations. "If I go with the guy who gives the lowest price today," my friend asks, "what happens tomorrow when I need product and there is a shortage? Who comes to my factory at midnight on Saturday to keep the production line running? The guy who sold the discount parts? Not likely." The willingness to ride out tough times in a business relationship means a real relationship must exist. If it does, the deals will follow.

In Harmony There Is Prosperity

The importance of establishing good interpersonal relationships is illustrated by the Japanese preoccupation with preserving *wa*, which means, quite literally, harmony. For the typical American manager, preserving company harmony is not a major preoccupation. For the Japanese, it is Job One.

According to a recent study performed by Accountemps, the world's largest clerical temporary personnel service, United States managers complain that they spend too much of their time, up to 13%, "resolving conflicts among workers." I know that before I came in contact with Japanese management styles I had the same complaint. My most pressing concern, as a business leader and manager, was making the numbers: reaching the sales targets and staying within budget. Virtually 99% of my stress revolved around worrying about the numbers, with very little of my time devoted to what seemed like "side issues" of company harmony. Like the managers cited in the Accountemps study, I had little patience and sometimes no toleration at all for dealing with issues like, is Joe happy with his job, does Mary like her desk or is Cindy a good supervisor. Such concerns seemed like diversions, petty issues that distract from the main tasks at hand. After all, I was hired to do the "real work"—to deliver the numbers.

In most Japanese companies, however, wa, harmony, is a foremost concern: It is real work. Japanese managers tell me that a majority of their personal stress, anywhere from 50 to 70%, is generated because of the need to manage wa and maintain harmony. My Japanese colleagues worry about making the numbers, too. But wa comes first.

Cultural, historic, and even geographic factors have led to the Japanese preoccupation with wa. On an island teeming with people, it is impossible to escape to the frontier and start a new life. In Japan, the frontier was a human one: how to find ways for millions of people to live together on an island devoid of substantial natural resources. Anthropologists, historians, and cultural geographers have filled volumes commenting on the development of the Japanese group mentality and identity. What matters here is not how the Japanese became what they are, but rather that what they are, at least as it concerns business management strategies, provides some tangible advantages. By creating a sense of group identity and loyalty, Japanese managers get more from their employees. A sense of the importance of wa is fundamental to the Japanese management style.

Perhaps the most vivid example I can recall of this Japanese sensitivity to wa involved the time my friend, Catholic priest Hugh Leonard left his position as leader of a human relations group in Hitachi-City, Japan. Prior to his departure he did something quite routine in a Western setting: He appointed his successor. It turned out to be a big mistake. For months after he left there was resentment and dissension among his former co-workers. One of Leonard's colleagues eventually explained that, in Japan at least, such personnel decisions were not to be made unilaterally.

For a new supervisor to have the support and cooperation of colleagues requires that each and every person be in some way involved or consulted prior to making the formal announcement of new leadership. It turns out, Leonard was later assured, that the group would have eventually picked the very same person that Leonard himself had selected for the top job. But the decision, if done Japanese-style, would have been the result of a harmonious group process and thus, would have been automatically respected and accepted. Unfortunately, because my friend was unaware of the subtleties of wa, it took his group a full six months before the new leader was able to restore the harmony that had been crippled by a unilateral and nonconsensual action.

Rather than viewing the pursuit of wa as a burden, it should be viewed as an opportunity. What often appear to be childish disputes over turf or feelings within a company, once settled, can clear the way for accomplishments that are magnified in scope and importance by the number of people who participate and contribute fully to the undertakings of the group. Once again, it is easy to take this practice too far by seeking total group harmony on every issue all the time, as sometimes happens in Japan. In reality, achieving wa is not as important as making a sincere effort in that direction. Everyone may not agree. But if attention is paid to these issues, at least everyone feels they have been properly consulted and treated with respect by their colleagues and supervisors.

Managing the Person—The Whole Person

Perhaps the most impressive attribute of skilled managers is the amount of information they typically know about individual employees. While workers in Japan usually avoid bringing personal problems up at work, most Japanese managers are keenly interested in learning more about an individual employee's home life and personal interests.

This information is valuable on several levels. Simply showing an interest in an employee's personal life is a powerful way for a manager to convey status to that person; it demonstrates that what the employee cares about is also important to the manager. In addition, knowing the pressures an individual must cope with, whether it is an ill child or parent or housing problems, gives the supervisor a better chance of understanding the particular needs and capabilities of an employee.

Rather than waiting for crises to erupt over personal problems, successful managers anticipate such crises by continually getting to know the people they are managing. In Japan, most of this familiarization happens in informal socializing after work, but also during the work day, at lunch or in those few minutes before a formal business meeting gets underway. In Japan, when an employee gets in trouble or experiences some family trauma, even during off-hours, the supervisor feels a personal responsibility to help. For example, if an employee is having trouble with his spouse the Japanese supervisor will often offer counsel and whatever help, advice, and support he can. Help offered when it is most needed is help remembered.

In Japan, most of these "whole person" interactions are of a decidedly more positive nature. For example, a manager I know learned of an employee's interest in vintage automobiles. The manager made a point of having his secretary locate car museums near any of the employee's travel destinations and, when possible, built time into the employee's schedule to allow a visit to the collections. Similar personalized fringe benefits, like memberships at golf courses, access to favorite restaurants, or attendance at favorite sporting events are often the product of a Japanese manager's knowledge of the whole person.

Providing these customized bonuses that employees cherish but would rarely buy for themselves is an enormous morale booster. Anyone can give a cash bonus, and Japanese employees do expect performance-based cash rewards, but the more personalized bonus—the great restaurant, the round of golf, or the visit to the auto museum—are rewards that linger in an employee's consciousness a bit longer and strengthen the human bonds that unify a successful organization. Managing the whole person is the best way to get that person, all of that person, fully engaged in his or her job. This is one area where most managers would do well to move their behavior closer to the classic Japanese model.

Managing the whole person is so important to the Japanese that there are even words in the Japanese language that refer specifically to the degree to which real, honest communication is taking place in a business relationship.

I remember, for example, hearing about one particularly vexing negotiating session between a major Japanese company and Alcoa Aluminum, the giant American combine. It was late in the evening and the talks were going nowhere, each side stating over and over again the positions they had opened the meeting with. In frustration, one of the Americans suggested the group knock off for the night and get a fresh start in the morning.

"No," replied the Japanese adversary, "let's go out for a drink." After several hours marinating their opinions in a local bar, the adversaries were soon singing together and slapping one another's backs, in classic Japanese *karaoke* style. Stumbling, arm in arm, into a cab after the late night session, the two main negotiators spoke no business. Instead, they talked about personal matters, their career hopes, the accomplishments of their children, recreational pursuits, and family life.

In the morning, when the negotiations were reconvened, there was a sudden movement in the stalled negotiations— movement on both sides. The relationship had deepened, from what the Japanese call the *tatemae*, the formal stance or even the facade, to the *honne*, or the genuine "inside" and more honest position. In reality, it was the meeting after the meeting that mattered most.

Listening to tatemae positions is a bit like reading the standard business letter. Business letters usually mean what they say but often do not say all they really mean. The Japanese are keenly aware that there are at least two channels of communication between individuals. There is what can be properly said in public and there is what is felt, and sometimes passed along, in private.

The word "tatemae" has its roots in an ancient Japanese word that connotes the outer or visible layer of something. It is a metaphysical orientation to the truth that holds there is an outer truth, tatemae, and an inner truth, honne. Similarly, the word "honne" has its roots in a Japanese word that means "the origin of sound," the true or most heartfelt motivation. This duality of truth, tatemae and honne, and the fact that the Japanese have precise words with which to differentiate the concepts, illustrates the more finely developed Japanese pattern of interpersonal communication.

In the honne mode, it becomes possible to find out what makes other people tick, what their real motivations are, what they actually expect, and what their real plans are. For the Japanese, switching into the honne mode takes some time and is usually not done in a formal business meeting. It does not have to be done in a bar, either, although in Japan that is the usual setting. However, if you want to do business with someone, or manage more effectively, or conduct any kind of negotiations, it is desirable, even necessary, that you get to know the whole person, not just that narrow slice related to your business objective.

That is why, in Japan, there are two business days: one that starts at 8:30 A.M. and runs until 7 P.M. and one that starts at 7 P.M. and runs until 10 P.M. It is that last business day, when the workers are in the honne mode, which dictates much of what happens during the formal business day. Once again, the emphasis is on creating and nurturing relationships.

I have traveled to Japan about 50 times in the past several years, staying there for about a week on each occasion. Upon arrival, I quickly get into the routine of the two business days. Like the Alcoa executives, my business meetings during the day are often full of contention and difficult business negotiations. At night, however, we almost always go out and work just as hard at getting to know each other, delving into the essential human character of each other.

Typically, our first stop during the evening or "second business day" is a Japanese restaurant where we take our time, two hours or more, over a leisurely dinner. Then we wander off to a karaoke or *ginza* hostess bar. At the Japanese hostess bars, the well-trained hostesses enhance communication among the group they serve by keeping all the drinks full and the jokes laughed at. More than anything else, the hostesses, who are often mischaracterized in Western accounts, are there to keep the conversation lubricated and pleasant. Frequently, we visit more than one hostess bar per evening, as different bars, due to their lighting and noise levels, facilitate different types of communication. The Japanese business days are unbelievably long and arduous. I have often wondered how they manage to keep up with it all. But these long hours and constant interactions certainly build strong relationships and a deep understanding of the honne aspects of interpersonal business relationships.

When I joined Toshiba America, I recall being struck by something my supervisor, Mr. Harai, said. After hearing that his corresponding senior manager in Tokyo, Mr. Satoh, was being moved to Europe and would be replaced by another senior manager, Mr. Harai expressed his dismay. "I worked with Mr. Satoh so long and I know him so well that I know how and what he is thinking before he formally communicates it to me," he said with obvious fondness. This is a unique way of looking at communicating and working with colleagues. How do they reach this level of communication? A few two-day work days, complete with full evening drinking sessions, helped me resolve this mystery.

Western managers, and particularly U.S. business executives, often tend to neglect the personal, holistic side of their colleagues. Predisposed to my own culturally imposed task-orientation, I have often been told by my Japanese colleagues to lighten up, for example, by not talking business during a golf match or at dinner; this is "personal time," they politely remind me. The honne mode facilitates business by ignoring it. Instead, an effort is made to get to know the real person behind the business facade. It is all about building up the trust that makes for good business relationships.

Westerners tend to want to write everything down, in a contract, a letter of agreement, or some formal document. The Japanese want instead to develop a sense of trust, a sense of honest intentions and honorable behavior. With that sense intact, all the other items, the ones an American or European would put in a contract or a job description, become what they are: mere details.

Once again, the art of the relationship comes before the art of the deal. Not surprisingly, a recent study of document intensity in Japanese and American businesses revealed that U.S. business generates, on average, 20 pieces of paper for every one generated by the Japanese. You simply don't have to bother to write things down if everyone already knows about them.

It is clearly unrealistic for managers to make a Japanese-style five-night-a-week effort at getting to know the personal side of business colleagues. But most Western managers can certainly do more than they do today. Interestingly, many of the best sales professionals already grasp the importance of this type of relationship-building; just ask their sometimes neglected spouses. However, this approach is not for sales professionals only. All managers, especially top executives and project directors, would benefit from strengthening their work-related personal relationships. Getting to know and understand colleagues is vital.

At Seiko Instruments, USA, for example, we recently convened a two-day off-site strategic planning session for one of our business groups. Senior management from both sides of the Pacific were represented. Repeatedly, I implored the Japanese managers to share their honne feelings with us. Simply recognizing that the honne channel exists helped break the ice with our Japanese colleagues, who then started to speak more freely.

However, our next session was scheduled to take place in Japan at the onsen (hot springs) where, in Japanese style, the workplace retreat is a much more highly refined and even more productive activity. Typically, we sit together naked in a hot bath, communicating "belly to belly," then share dinner in a communal small dining room which, later that evening, becomes the group bedroom. This arrangement does a lot to create trust and a sense of teamwork.

Many Western companies recognize the importance of getting to know the whole person they are dealing with only in the recruitment phase. Once people have been hired, an invitation to dine or drink with the boss is a coveted, although sometimes feared, event. For the Japanese such informal interactions are routine. The Japanese even have a phrase, *honne de ikimasho*, which means, literally, "let's go into the honne mode," which they will often say as they go out in the evening. Consciously, they invite each other to deepen their relationships by encouraging communication on a more personal and sincere level.

At Seiko Instruments, USA, I tested ways of moving my workforce closer to the honne mode. For example, I participated in a fair amount of symbolic dinners, at least one per month. Usually, after hitting an important milestone in a particular project, or at some other regular interval, I would invite a group of employees to be entertained at company expense. In deference to family and commuter concerns, it was usually an early dinner at a nearby Chinese restaurant, where the shared dishes further enhanced the cohesiveness of the group. We made this such a regular practice it almost felt like a regular family event.

In addition, I invite employees to join me on short car trips around town, to participate together in community events, and to join our company sports teams. Although we have a long way to go to equal the degree of Japanese honne-style interactions, these efforts seem to be paying off in enhanced teamwork, communication, and productivity.

The Honorable Approach

Giri is another Japanese term with no direct English equivalent. It refers to what North Carolina State University professor Linda S. Dillon calls "a range of obligation" or what Japan scholar Edward Hall describes as "indebtedness to others." In my experience, giri is almost always a positive force; it is what remains after business or personal relationships have deepened through exchanges of mutual trust and appreciation. Occasionally, only after some grave personal offense has been committed, giri takes on a negative, "getting even" connotation. Usually, however, the need to get even because of giri refers to the duty to do something nice, like return a compliment.

For example, explains Dillon, "If I recommend you for a job, you feel giri toward me. If you want to leave that company, I am part of your relationship to it, and you must consult with me first." Similarly, once two companies start doing business together, Dillon notes, "It is against giri for one company to drop the other without very good reason."

When, for example, I felt enough giri toward Mr. Harai, who hired me into Toshiba and provided me with significant support while I was there, I deemed it necessary to consult with him and, in effect, to ask his permission to seriously consider the opportunity offered me at Seiko Instruments, USA. By that time, Mr. Harai had himself left Toshiba and was then president of Digital Research, Japan, so it made it a little easier for him to favorably consider my request. But my giri obligation dictated that, regardless of the circumstances, I consult with Mr. Harai in order to preserve and honor the relationship we had cultivated independently of our association with Toshiba.

Giri is the result of all Japanese relationship-building. It is that palpable, yet intangible, sense of personal honor, the "I can't do that to so-and-so because we have giri between us" attitude, or, "of course I'll come in and work on Sunday to help my colleague, with whom I have a relationship built on giri." The goal of Japanese manager and worker alike is to build and maintain giri, a pattern of honorable interactions, as widely as possible.

Western managers might well ask themselves what they or their companies can do to create among their employees the sense of personal honor, of giri, which serves the Japanese so well. It is crucial to have employees, and customers when possible, bound to one another by some higher moral force. This may mean occasionally foregoing a business or management opportunity to make a fast buck if the opportunity comes at the expense of a customer, business partner, or employee. The essential strength of giri is that it grows out of an individual's sense of self-esteem and esteem for others. In Japan, giri sometimes feels like a socially regimented emotion, lacking in warmth, but its existence is a manifestation of profound loyalty. Once the giri mentality is established, it acts as an internal regulator and helps lead workers and managers to treat each other as longtime allies.

In Japan, a person's failure to honor any one giri relationship can damage all similar relationships. The person is quickly labeled and shunned as an unappreciative ingrate or a coward, afraid or unable to take the socially proper action. For this reason, Japanese managers often fail to understand the behavior of some non-Japanese employees, who may be totally unaware of giri expectations, such as those created when one is offered and accepts a job. In workplaces in which giri is not second-nature it is important for managers to actively model the desired behavior.

For instance, as is usually the case, the power of management's example is huge; when workers see their managers respect and honor their own longstanding business relationships it creates a heightened desire among employees to develop similar relationships, both within the company and between themselves and outside suppliers or customers.

A young employee who witnesses his supervisor honoring a longstanding business relationship or obligation gets a powerful message from that interaction; it demonstrates that, to the manager, each individual relationship is important and, potentially, long-lasting. It lets employees know, almost subconsciously, that they also have an opportunity to develop such mutually reciprocal and beneficial relationships with their co-workers, managers, and subordinates. Modeling this behavior is perhaps the best way a manager can reinforce the sense that success in business is directly linked with each employee's relationships with customers and colleagues.

For example, I recently had an opportunity to start a new relationship with a major Japanese consumer electronics vendor. First, we met in my office to review progress on our product development activities. Then we played golf. Golf was followed by dinner at my house, punctuated with an end-of-evening picture-taking session. The next day, after a one-hour wrap-up meeting in my office, my guest hosted me for dinner at one of his favorite restaurants. Outside the office, very little business was discussed. However, when my guest departed we both had the feeling of being long-lost buddies. We could have, of course, concluded our business discussions in far less time. Instead, we took the time to get it right; both of us now feel a responsibility to help each other in ways we might not have considered if our personal relationship was not as strong. On a less intense basis, I try to nurture similar relationships with all of my key business contacts. Doing so improves the working relationship and, in addition, helps make business much more pleasant and enjoyable.

Relationship-building is perhaps the most compelling and satisfying part of doing business Japanese-style. In a highly effective and culturally unique way, many of the Japanese I have worked with over the years have won permanent places in my heart; I have fond memories of many of these individuals and a strong sense of giri exists between us. For the Japanese, relationship-building is, indeed, a daily practice, honed to a high art. Within limits, most managers would do well to learn to apply this artful approach to human relationships.

The Alchemist's Tool Kit #3
Art of the Relationship Checklist

AMERICAN/WESTERN	JAPANESE
Work the deal before the relationship in most business functions	Work the relationship before the deal in all business functions
Confrontation	Compromise
Deal with the position/person	Deal with the person/position
Little stress is placed on harmony and wa	A lot of stress is placed on harmony and wa
Often unwilling to commit time to get to know the whole person	Invest considerable time in getting to know the whole person; build honne channels of communication
Emphasis on ability/character	Emphasis on character/ability

MANAGEMENT TIPS

• Work the relationship before working the deal. Forget the short-term deal or sale; concentrate on establishing long-term relationships first. This applies to all functions in business, not only sales.

• Encourage employees to build strategic relationships with customer and supplier by attending open houses and other events.

• One of management's most important tasks is nurturing and maintaining wa (harmony) within the company.

- Manage the person—the whole person. Take responsibility for managing your subordinates by accepting any failure of a subordinate as your own failure.

- Understand honne and tatemae communication channels. Keep the honne channel clear and open with dinners, sports, and shared experiences.

- Understand the concept of having two business days, 8:00–7:00 and 7:00–10:00. Selectively, use that "second business day" to build relationships and teamwork.

- Create giri, a sense of honor in your organization, by always acting honorably with employees, vendors, community, and customers.

- Understand the continuum of human relationships. Move all important business relationships closer to the Japanese or ROW (rest of the world) model.

4

A COLLECTIVE
IDENTITY:

Blending the Company
"We" and the Individual "I"

John Sculley, the former chairman of Apple Computer, knows quite a bit about blending the strengths of Western and Japanese business management practices. Initially, Apple faltered in Japan's tough computer market. Unlike the quick success the company enjoyed in the United States, for a painfully long time competitors like NEC and IBM made Apple's prospects in Japan an open question. Because of the unique design of Apple products and the intentionally mystical nature of the company, luring topflight Japanese talent to Apple Japan posed considerable problems. The company's leaders found it difficult to find skilled Japanese programmers and technicians ready to gamble their careers on a potentially unstable American computer start-up company, even one as successful and well-known as Apple. Early on, the shortage of interested local recruits forced Apple Japan to hire Americans, many of them Japanese-Americans, to work at Apple Japan.

Then something happened. It would not have amounted

to much in most business settings, but in Japan it had enormous meaning. Sculley promoted Mr. Shay Takeuchi, Apple Japan's managing director, to the post of vice president, for the *U.S.* corporation. The move elevated Takeuchi to the high-status position held by only a handful of Apple executives.

At most companies, the promotion would have been viewed as an individual accomplishment. In Japan, however, it signaled that the whole group, all of Apple Japan, had been accorded full status in the Apple U.S. headquarters.

"It energized the entire workforce," says Lee Collins, a veteran Apple Asia hand. "It was as if they had all been promoted to vice president. The employees took the promotion very seriously." And suddenly, according to Takeuchi, recruiting employees became much easier.

This sense of collective identity is an extension of kaizen principles, which emphasize process issues. By focusing constantly on the performance of the group, and by establishing mechanisms that encourage and reward harmonious group interactions, it is possible to inculcate a sense of collective identity into a company culture. As Apple's Lee Collins notes, the sense of collective identity in Japan is so powerful that events that would have little or no effect elsewhere, like the promotion of a manager to VP level, have, in Japan, considerable consequences for the entire organization.

Insiders and Outsiders

Establishing a collective identity is a crucial step in building an effective business team. Japan's cohesive culture contributes to this sense of collective identity; the ethnically homogeneous Japanese society, organized around generally egalitarian values, leaves workers and managers acutely aware of the invisible line between insiders and outsiders.

Seiko Instruments former president, Ichiro Hattori, illustrated this point when he spoke to a class at MIT in 1988. "In Japan," Hattori noted, "Seiko's male regular employees, who form the core of the corporate employee community, work continuously as a group, and no differences are felt in standing among such groups." Mr. Hattori continued. "Very few people in top management ranks have been recruited from outside organizations . . . and employees as individuals maintain very little or no exchanges with outside organizations."

Hattori's comment does not reflect satisfaction with this state of affairs. In fact, he points out, the single largest advantage many non-Japanese businesses now enjoy over their Japanese counterparts stems from the essentially closed Japanese system Hattori describes. The wide-open culture in the United States, occasionally derided by some Japanese leaders, is nonetheless admired in Japan, particularly in business circles. When Japanese leaders aim a critical comment at Western culture it is generally targeted at the Western workforce and, in particular, the usual United States managerial style. For markets, however, most Japanese executives focus their primary export attention on the United States market, with the size of that market only part of the reason. Even more important is the pattern of (relative) xenophilia in the United States; whether it is foreign cars, foreign food, foreign music, or foreigners in general, Americans, more than most, have a tradition of welcoming outside influences and even incorporating them into the mainstream culture.

The Japanese, on the other hand, have a long history of insularity. Japan's most impressive success, the establishment of unified, team-oriented companies, is, of course, in part a result of this insularity. The emphasis on human relationships, group performance improvements, honne communications, and giri, combined with the ethnically homogeneous Japanese society, contribute to this strong collective identity which, on the negative side, can sometimes discourage or even intimidate outsiders.

Usually, the Japanese develop this concept of the insider early on, starting with the family, then the school, then the company, and then the country, perhaps, some allege, in the reverse order. The result is a very tight "old boy" network, which makes it hard for an outsider to be accepted. This attitude, carried to its extreme, may be Japan's fatal flaw.

Mr. Hattori, a member of the family that founded the Seiko Group, describes the negative aspects of this total insider orientation. "In Japan," Hattori relates, "there are many cases in which enterprises, whose markets have reached a saturation point or whose business operations are technically deadlocked, have top management with experience in nothing but outmoded undertakings." The Japanese tendency to pull their wagons in a circle in such situations and to resist the influence of outsiders is "why such enterprises, in many cases, are late in triggering a switch-over and beckon tragedy by failing to ride the crest of the [latest] waves of innovation," Hattori noted. His strategy to reverse this process at Seiko Instruments included instructing employees on the necessity to allow new ideas, technology, and people to "parachute," as he was forced to call it, "into the company."

In traditional Japanese companies there are major constraints when it comes to hiring and absorbing professional expertise. Many Japanese companies simply will not hire people from other companies, outsiders, at higher-than-entry-level wage due to the dispiriting disruption this may create among the company's existing employees.

I saw this first hand at Toshiba when we entered the laser printer business. Other manufacturers, especially Canon, were already doing quite well in that market and a pool of talented and experienced people existed within those other companies whom Toshiba could have "cherry-picked." Instead of hiring some of these top engineers to speed the development of Toshiba's laser printing business the company decided to reinvent the wheel by utilizing its own staff of copier-trained engineers. Consequently, the development of Toshiba's laser printing products took much longer than was really required and, in this instance, the company ended up missing the window of opportunity on that market. It seemed my colleagues at Toshiba preferred to fail on their own rather than depend on others for success.

The heightened sense of "we" and "they" commonplace among Japanese employees owes some of its being to the career development process in Japan. Managers progress through their careers together at most major Japanese companies. I remember, for example, one of my senior managers at Toshiba referring to other managers in the company as his "classmates." Together they had entered the company, been trained, and in near lockstep moved up the corporate ladder. This is an extra bond; each group of people entering any major Japanese company is given a class year designation.

However, as Mr. Hattori and other leaders at Seiko Instruments have demonstrated, in part by placing Americans like me in senior positions, it isn't necessary to establish the traditional Japanese siege mentality, where outsiders are labeled, clearly identified, and often vilified, in order to reinforce the collective identity of the insider group, although that is certainly a commonplace method still employed in Japan.

On the contrary, I've learned that it is far more important to strengthen the collective identity by constantly measuring your group against the actual competition, not, as sometimes happens in Japan, the rest of the world. My experience with Japanese companies has taught me that building a sense of collective identity is crucial. My experience with American companies, however, has taught me that welcoming newcomers onto the team is the most practical way to expand this necessary sense of collective identity in today's global business environment.

With a known outside "enemy" it becomes easier to co-alesce the inside group and get them working together against the external threat. Energy is focused on understanding and beating the competition, not on the intramural squabbles within the company or between departments. Japanese companies sometimes go overboard in this regard, seeing their company as locked in battle with virtually everyone who does not work for their company. However, outside Japan, many companies do not pay enough attention to their competition.

Take, for instance, the classic example of the American auto industry. How many years did it take before Detroit took their Japanese competition seriously? Japanese auto companies, on the other hand, used comparative ads and competitive features early on to highlight the advantages of their products. Meanwhile, most American car companies took little or no public notice of the products that were beating them in the marketplace and continued to produce and advertise their wares as if no competition existed. Only recently has this situation changed. Today, many Detroit industry veterans freely credit the Japanese auto industry for forcing them into more market-oriented growth strategies.

Japanese auto executives, unlike those who led Detroit into decline, stayed focused on their competition; the competition were the outsiders who threatened the well-being of the inside Japanese group. They realized that to ignore the competition for even one moment was to put the health of their companies, and their own personal prosperity, in jeopardy.

The extreme displays of loyalty to the company within Japan are a manifestation of this "us against them" attitude. Occasionally, for example, when a company has suffered a setback, Japanese employees might appear to engage in a gnashing-of-teeth contest to see who can grieve more earnestly. The histrionics may be overdone by Western tastes, but the emotion is sincere. Japanese employees, although becoming more Westernized every day, still look on their companies as their lifeline. "The company," one Japanese executive told me, "is no substitute for the family, but it is what allows me to enjoy my family, to have my family, and to maintain the respect of my family."

While Westerners do not, for the most part, share the historical background of the agrarian Japanese, who for centuries were forced to cooperate closely in agricultural undertakings lest they all starve, it is still possible to emulate the positive aspects of establishing and maintaining a strong sense of collective identity. This can and should be done without going to extremes. In particular, there is no need to exclude potentially necessary people and ideas from the team you establish.

Taking full advantage of the opportunity to build an expanding sense of group identity requires some understanding of cultural factors, both for Westerners and for Japanese. For example, loners, the classic American heroes, have little if any sense of collective identity. In Japan, however, to be a loner means, more often than not, that one has been ostracized and shamed. American workers are not motivated to the same degree by the subtle terror of ostracization commonplace in Japan. But there are practical techniques, more positive and reinforcing in nature, that enable workers to create a sense of group identity, a sense of being an insider, even within the individualistic American culture.

As a manager, I'm always looking for opportunities to build the collective identity of our group through company newsletters, informal sports competitions, hosted dinners, and the like. While these activities are often seen in the United States as distractions from the real work of the company, in reality, these activities offer the best hope of creating an environment in which more of the real work actually gets done. Often, insofar as building a sense of collective identity goes, how the work gets done can be even more important than what actually gets accomplished. The managerial techniques that follow are of particular help in this regard.

Fix the Problem Not the Blame

Early in my career, I had many difficult and stressful encounters with my Japanese colleagues, particularly when we reviewed countermeasures to reverse negative variances to our budget. At Toshiba, for example, my American managers and I spent our first year or so really knocking ourselves out. We had a new, non-IBM compatible personal computer the market did not want; we could not make any changes without getting engineering in Japan to approve and implement them; and management in Japan did not fully understand the U.S. market. The budget called for $3 million in sales in the first six months. We shipped almost that much equipment that year, but when we were unable to make the engineering upgrades we had promised, most of the product came right back to our loading dock.

I was doing the best I could under the circumstances, but I readied myself for big trouble as I prepared to meet with my Japanese higher-ups. They represented manufacturing, product development, and finance, and I represented sales and marketing. Everyone was under stress. We were not "making our numbers" and I knew something had to be done. I prepared myself for a knock-down-drag-out fight over who was to blame for our lousy performance.

But the donnybrook never happened. When we got together to talk about why we were underperforming no one got emotional. The discussions were calm, and the focus was always on solving the problem. Rather than chastising me and putting me on the defensive, the higher-ups talked about what was going wrong and how to fix it. I was surprised—and greatly relieved.

When we came up short at Toshiba, there was no finger-pointing session. Instead, my Japanese managers quickly made it clear: They wanted to fix the problem, not the blame. There were no accusations hurled at colleagues, no "I told you so's," no whispered insults in the hall. Instead, there was a concerted effort to solve the problems.

Immediately, I felt I was part of a team and suddenly found myself working that much harder to get us out of our predicament. I realized that others in the company had a lot of trust in me, and I wanted to live up to that.

I can't help but think what might have happened. When things go wrong, our natural reflex is to find a scapegoat. At another company, I might have been fired and replaced. And the problems would still have been there for the new person to deal with.

Because of routine maintenance of the collective identity, this kind of thing does not happen very often in Japanese businesses. The Japanese are much less likely to believe that getting rid of or adding one new person will make much of a difference. By fixing the blame, a manager assumes that the problem is with an individual. By concentrating on fixing the problem, the manager and worker assume the problem is with the process and they work together to improve re-sults—a tactic that often improves individual performance as well.

Over the years, I've found it practical to work under the assumption that everyone is working hard and doing their best. To do otherwise is to create a culture of perpetual in-sults and attacks on the character of employees and col-leagues. My strategy, based on my combined Japanese and American perspective, is to work very hard on enhancing results by understanding and changing the underlying situation. In the United States, a football coach has one losing season and he is out on the street. In Japan, firing an employee constitutes a failure of grave proportions. Of course, Japan's strong company labor unions make it practically impossible to fire an employee in the usual U.S. fashion.

The Japanese management style is more of a family-type relationship. As in a family, the assumption is that each member is a permanent part of the group. This stems from the once common Japanese custom of lifetime employment with one company. Although fewer than one-third of Japanese male employees work for the large companies that virtually promise lifetime employment, this job-for-life custom remains the template for Japanese people management. The employee is presumed to be a permanent member of the group. Thus, real emphasis is placed on preserving an employee's sense of personal dignity. Problems are solved in an informal, face-saving atmosphere whenever possible.

For the Japanese, to blame someone within the company for a failure constitutes a failure by the person placing the blame. Pointing a finger at someone else is considered lazy, at best, and shows a basic incompetence, the inability to work with others.

Many of my non-Japanese colleagues wonder how difficult business decisions are made in this extraordinarily polite and deferential environment. In fact, this polite environment, which focuses on problems rather than personalities, can be very effective since, in tough settings, full communication cannot take place if there are strong emotions, anger, or personal animosities.

As a manager armed with the experience of working in Japanese companies, I've come to have little use for criticism aimed at individual personalities. When we have a problem with an employee, especially a manager, I'm reminded of the most common response from my Japanese colleagues: "We must help that person." Firing the employee is usually not an option, and is never the first option; moving the person to another job in the company is often the most extreme action contemplated in most Japanese companies. And this would only happen at the beginning of a fiscal period, in April or October, so that an appearance of it being an orderly, face-saving transition can be maintained.

In Japan, even when an employee goes into the penalty box it is done subtly. A year or two, or longer, in the penalty box is what befalls a manager who is responsible for a major failure. Unlike outside Japan, where that manager is likely to be put out in the street, the Japanese penalty box is a temporary demotion. After a few years spent servicing accounts or compiling paperwork, the penalized manager, who is still invited to the important company meetings, usually gets a chance to redeem himself or herself. This clear penalty with chance of later recovery serves to reinforce the sense of collective identity and helps develop a good organization. People make mistakes. If it becomes known within an organization that mistakes are not fatal, it is possible to avoid the fear-induced group paralysis so common in dysfunctional organizations. Liberated from the fear of being cast out, employees feel more free to experiment, to think more independently, and to act more decisively.

Managers should apply this technique whenever possible by making the phrase "fix the problem and not the blame" part of their company's culture. Working through problems and maintaining long-term relationships within an organization is ultimately more profitable than constantly changing people and partners. The only way to establish this culture, and to encourage people to fix processes rather than hide problems, is to show by example that people do not get "beat up" when there is a problem. In the U.S. economy, where short-term pressures often result in layoffs and take-overs, only those companies who manage to maintain the loyalty of their most precious human resource teams have any real hope of long-term survival.

I remember, for example, one executive who helped engineer the takeover of a major U.S. advertising agency only to discover that internal squabbling had led many key individuals to leave the organization. "We bought the company," he remarked, "but the assets went down the elevator one night and never came back." Laying off people, usually a last resort in Japan, should never be a first resort anywhere. Those human resources, if sent down the elevator with instructions not to come back, are like squandered investments.

On the other hand, fixing the problem and not the blame enhances teamwork and offers the hope that difficult times might be surmounted. This requires keeping the focus on the process rather than on the personalities as much as possible. With this goal in mind, I frequently remind my managers that one of their most serious responsibilities is to build a workplace culture in which personal attacks are not tolerated and problems and processes are fixed rather than blame assessed.

Team-Building: The Nail That Stands Up Gets Pounded Down

A well-known Japanese saying goes "the nail that stands up gets pounded down," which, of course, sounds like a quite repressive situation. The phrase however, reflects the Japanese preoccupation with enhancing the work process within the group rather than lionizing any one individual worker. In Japan, the most frequent form of employee recognition usually revolves around celebrating the years of service to a company, rather than any individual accomplishment, like sales per month. The emphasis is always on nurturing the sense of collective identity. I always try to combine this Japanese-style reticence, team-orientation, and personal modesty with the typically more innovative American individualistic approach.

Pounding down employees who stand up, or who stand out, can, of course, be counterproductive. In addition, it is largely unnecessary if the goal is to enhance group solidarity and thereby increase total group productivity. Something is lost when individuals are forced to submerge their identities into a group and I don't recommend this approach without some qualification. But what is gained—the strengthening of the group—is of enough value that it is worth exploring how Western reliance on independence and individualism can be harnessed within the framework of the group identity.

For example, I often encourage my managers to work hard at celebrating small wins on a frequent basis. Typically, they'll convene their work groups for a 30-minute recognition event. Chocolate cookies and milk are passed around and individual workers are given credit for accomplishments, even modest ones, that have some corporatewide significance. A few of the employees will be given a chance to talk about what they did and to thank their colleagues. This allows for individual recognition in the context of group recognition. In addition, the bonus objectives for all of my senior managers include measurable group goals; my managers are evaluated in large part by how well their entire team performs. If the team meets the manager's bonus goals, typically at the end of a six-month evaluation period, there is usually another celebration, this one larger, hosted by the appreciative manager.

Hiroshi Fukind, one of my Japanese colleagues at Seiko Instruments illustrated the value of this approach when he pointed out that "people have to realize the limitations of what one person can do in today's business world. If they could do everything themselves, there would be no need to form an organization or a business." My friend explained that, like many Japanese, he learned this lesson in his childhood, as it was imparted by parents, schoolmates, and teachers. His summary of these basic lessons, which he learned while American children were busy watching the Lone Ranger, are as follows:

- You can be successful, but not by yourself.
- You must get along with your colleagues to be successful.
- Life is long. Sometimes you must let your opponents win. That way, they may provide you with an opportunity to win later.
- You cannot always be a winner. History explains that winners and losers change places frequently.
- You will never truly know the value of winning unless you know the bitterness of losing. Don't be afraid of losing, especially when you are young. Remember, life is long.

My experience tells me that these attitudes are commonplace among Japanese managers. Through their early education Japanese are taught the value of teamwork, that they are only as good as the team they are part of, and that ultimately, they will be judged by how well they worked with others. Even when an individual is rewarded for a business success with a promotion, colleagues are likely to be given heartfelt credit for the accomplishment. "I was just lucky," the promoted Japanese worker will say most sincerely. And his colleagues will likely agree, feeling that next time around the luck might just fall their way.

I've even seen this attitude at work on golf courses in Japan. When a Japanese golfer hits a hole-in-one the custom is to "redistribute" their portion of unearned luck by buying gifts, meals, and drinks for all colleagues. Japanese golfers actually take out hole-in-one insurance to cover the costs of these rare redistributions of link luck. The miraculous individual accomplishment represented by a hole-in-one leaves Japanese golfers feeling uneasy and compels them to reinforce and strengthen their identification with their group. When confronted with this type of unearned luck, Japanese will often say that "evil is smiling on them." Realizing the unpredictability of their good fortune they will assume practically no credit for their accomplishment.

In business, this attitude can help ward off disaster. For example, I currently sit on the board of a small American software company that is enjoying fabulous success with strong sales growth and very strong profits. The company has quickly become the leading supplier in an important industrial niche market. The future looks very bright. However, I repeatedly remind them that this extraordinary success is really "evil smiling on them." More precisely, fast sales growth and high profit margins cover up a host of sins.

Rather than bask in their success, I urge them to keep looking at their operations, and challenge them to expand their sales globally, and improve their procedures. Sooner or later, as most Japanese managers routinely expect, their luck will change and their success "nail," sticking up so proudly, will get pounded. It is healthy, I believe, to understand the role of luck in business and, if anything, to overstate rather than overlook its importance. If you do well because you were lucky you still have an obligation to work hard. If you think you have done well because you are good, the work output may slow and the success soon evaporate like so much unearned and random luck.

In Japan, new employees usually fit themselves quietly into the group so as not to be "a nail that stands up." Instead, they hold back and slowly fit in. By doing so, an employee shows respect for the group he or she is entering. For example, while it is possible for a newcomer to suggest ideas and have them implemented, a "strategic options memo" circulated to supervisors on the first day of work is more likely to antagonize than impress. While the outsider may have the answers the company needs, portraying those answers as the sole product of one person's work upsets the group process. Instead, the Japanese have made a tradeoff: in exchange for occasional moments of greatness from individual superstars they have substituted the steady progress of a cohesive, unified group. And in business, consistency is a more certain path to survival.

To strike the right balance and make optimal use of this powerful Japanese management technique, I often remind those who work with me that our company has no heroes—and no bums. If the company wins, everyone wins. If the company loses, everyone loses. Any time spent fixing individual blame or looking for personal credit is time taken away from making the group work as effectively and harmoniously as possible.

I've tested this approach and found it to be a productive middle ground between the Japanese tactic of "pounding the nail that stands up" and the American tendency to pay attention only to those who stand out. For that reason, I encourage my managers and employees to realize that a great idea is only a great idea if as many people as possible are involved in its development and implementation.

The Value of Consistency: Flexible Rigidity

Another major difference between Western and Japanese management styles revolves around the issue of consistency. As a rule, Westerners often seem to flit from idea to idea, frequently shifting course and changing strategy. The Japanese, on the other hand, tend more often to work longer on developing and refining an original idea and are then quite reluctant to change course once the plan is being implemented. It is like the difference between improvisational theater, similar to the Western business approach, and the more carefully scripted and directed Japanese performances, which can be replicated again and again.

The advantage of the Japanese approach is that it leads people to work harder at getting the better idea in place first and then communicating that idea to associates and colleagues. When, for example, I present my Japanese colleagues with a "better idea" of some sort, I have learned to expect the typical response: "But one month ago, you said such and such. Why are you changing now?" For them, the value of a new idea is always judged, in part, by the damage implementing that new idea may cause to the organization's carefully cultivated prior plans. In fact, one of the first criticisms I received from my Japanese colleagues was that I changed my business plans too often. The people behind you, I was told, are like a stack of dominoes and as you change direction the whole stack falls back. This criticism, like others, can be taken too far. However, the essential lesson is valuable for many non-Japanese managers.

One way to minimize this problem is to make sure to trace the development of any new idea from its roots in the old idea. I always try, when proposing a new idea to superiors, colleagues, and subordinates, to carefully and explicitly define what has occurred that has moved me from the old idea to the new one. Step by step, I carefully explore this line of reasoning, making sure to note the changed circumstances that have influenced my thinking. This exercise helps the entire work team evaluate whether a change is really necessary and, if so, builds support for the new undertaking. It is demoralizing for employees to be told to stop doing something if they do not understand why. Logically, they will approach the next task with a reduced sense of urgency, feeling that seemingly capricious decisions might soon make even their best efforts meaningless.

In addition, a consistent, low tolerance for change forces people to invest time, effort, and resources toward getting the best idea in place right from the start. While opportunities for subsequent improvement may be diminished by a strict adherence to an original plan, this dynamic compels employees to avoid the "we'll fix it later" mentality. Using this approach, later is too late.

A McKinsey and Company study on bringing new products to market illustrates the benefits of a consistent approach. The McKinsey researchers determined that a significant reason some companies can quickly get products to market is so simple it is often overlooked: Companies that make fewer changes to a product concept once the development cycle starts usually beat their less decisive competition to the market. While this approach does occasionally lead to the implementation of ideas that are merely "good" rather than "the best," it avoids the continual changes of course that can cause an organization to lose its sense of direction. In an organization the premium should always be placed on consistency. Flexibility is also important, but not the impulsive variety. Changes should occur only after a careful and rational appraisal of the value of the proposed change. Improvisational theater is occasionally entertaining. Shakespeare, like Kabuki, is almost always a good show.

Alchemist's Tool Kit #4
Winning with People Checklist

AMERICAN/WESTERN	JAPANESE
Individual identity	Collective identity
Unique	Harmony
Independent	Dependent
"We" is the department	"We" is the company

MANAGEMENT TIPS

- Establish a collective identity for your company: no "you," no "I," just "we."

- Look for every opportunity to build a company-wide team of insiders with a collective identity.

- Focus on outside competition as the "enemy," not other departments within your organization.

- Forget about fixing the blame and create a culture of fixing the problem.

- Fixing the blame concentrates on an individual while fixing the problem concentrates on the process.

- Create a culture in which there are neither heroes nor bums. If the company wins everybody wins.

- Celebrate small wins on a frequent and modest basis.

- Schedule organizational changes at the beginning of a new fiscal year. If you have a six-month fiscal period, you have a chance to do this twice a year.

- If you are fortunate to have a good string of business suc-cesses, understand that some of this is excessive luck, or "evil smiling at us." A healthy dose of skepticism is good for your business attitude.

- Be consistent; do not change course too often. Then care-fully explain what events happened to cause the changes from the original plan.

5

THE WA FACTORY:

A Highly Empowered Personnel Department

Sony's factory in San Diego was one of the first postwar Japanese-owned factories operating in the United States. Initially, the factory managed to achieve an average performance based on American standards. However, compared with similar-sized factories in Japan, something was wrong. Production levels lagged behind Japanese targets, quality control was a problem, and absenteeism, almost unheard of in Japan, was commonplace.

Within two years, however, it all turned around. Production, quality control, and absenteeism approached, and then equaled, the levels attained in Japan. The turnaround was so startling that scholars at MIT undertook a study to determine what had happened. No, Sony did not import workers from Japan to replace the Americans. But Sony did import one thing the MIT scholars say helped make the difference: an effective and empowered personnel management system and department. Indeed, one of the very best ways to build a sense of collective identity in your ranks is to make optimum use of the company personnel department or personnel manager.

It may surprise Westerners to learn that the most important department in a Japanese company is usually not the research and development department, or the marketing department, or even the executive office. Instead, it is that often lowly backwater of most Western companies: the personnel department. For it is in the personnel department that strong people management policies within a company are formalized, monitored, and improved.

In most successful Japanese companies, the personnel department has considerable influence over an individual's career. Unlike many Western companies, in which the personnel department merely files employment applications and occasionally runs interference for the line managers who actually make the hire/fire decisions, the average Japanese personnel department is vested with considerable power. It is a power that serves to preserve wa, harmony, by letting employees and their bosses know that nothing going on in the company is done in a vacuum.

Personnel management in Japan is all about developing and enhancing conduits of communication—between the boss and the employee, but more vitally, between the employee and the company, as an entity apart from whoever their line boss might be. The admirable and intense Japanese communication ethic is so well-developed that it is actually built into the very structure of the Japanese workplace hierarchy.

"American bosses like to build little kingdoms," a friend of mine at Fujitsu group tells me. "They surround themselves with people who owe them their loyalty for having given them their job." A Japanese employee, on the other hand, owes his or her loyalty to the company. It was the company personnel department, in most cases, which hired the employee in the first place, so the welfare of the company stays foremost in the mind of the new hire. Employees are loyal to the company because the company, not any one individual, hired them. Employees know that the company trusts them to do what is right, regardless of who their immediate supervisor is.

This reliance on the personnel department to actually manage personnel, rather than just push paper around, extends all the way to the regular employee performance evaluations. At most major Japanese corporations only 15 to 40% of an employee's evaluation comes directly from the employee's supervisor. The majority of the evaluation comes from the personnel department, which looks at things such as the perception the company has of the employee's potential, the employee's performance in past assignments, the employee's performance in school, the level of education attained, communication skills, facility for teamwork, industriousness, after-work activities, education and training within the company, and creativity. The number of years an employee has been associated with the company are carefully noted and rated as an indication of the employee's value to the organization. Finally, evaluations from previous bosses are compared with the new evaluation to detect any differences that may be attributable to the bosses and not the employee.

The average Japanese personnel department is broadly concerned with maximizing an employee's potential within the company. If an employee gets a poor evaluation from the line supervisor but a good one from the personnel department, the onus is then placed squarely on the boss. If the employee is judged to have potential, has done well in other assignments or in school, then the problem, a Japanese manager may surmise, might rest with the supervisor and not the employee.

The Japanese ritual of performance evaluations thus takes on deep meaning and often actually enhances the performance of employees. Japanese performance evaluations provide the personnel department and the manager with much more information than the typical equivalent non-Japanese exercise. The Japanese learn if a boss-subordinate relationship is working, they learn if the personnel department might help a boss manage an employee more effectively, and the boss learns what the company expects from individual employees under his or her charge. Finally, employees learn that they are not alone and that if they are having a problem with an individual supervisor, the company wants to know about it and wants to help.

In most Japanese companies, when an employee and a boss fail to get along, the personnel department will step in and transfer the employee—or sometimes even the boss. Only after several such transfers will a Japanese company accept the fact that all the investments they have made in an employee were for naught. Often a Japanese manager will say, "We lost our investment in that person"—Japanese for "we fired him." And such comparatively rare events are considered almost as much a shame for the employer as the employee.

This structure reinforces the all-important sense of wa within a viable organization. Shorn of the power to terrify a subordinate through poor evaluations or threats of termination, the Japanese boss must instead find positive ways to motivate employees. The boss simply *must* communicate effectively, modifying the message until it gets through.

Similarly, the employee knows that her or his job is to serve the company, not build up the little empire of the boss. Many non-Japanese companies lose markets and squander opportunities while departments fight with each other like so many balkanized fiefdoms, each group owing its allegiance to individual power brokers in the company. It is not that Japanese fight with each other less than Westerners do; it is that, because of the genuine power of the personnel department, they have less to fight over. When the Japanese personnel management system is utilized, total communication within the group is enhanced and the boss and the employees only have to worry about one thing: getting the job done.

At Sony's San Diego plant, MIT scholars discovered that it was the personnel department's attention to little things that helped make the difference and enhance the factory's overall performance. Sony's personnel department, as is standard procedure in Japanese organizations, compiled extensive information on individual employees. Predictable things were included in the personnel files: employees' strengths, weaknesses, special skills, and the like. But other, more personal, things were also noted: the birthdays of employees' children, important upcoming school graduations, information on the health of an employee's parents, and so on.

As part of the personnel department's practice of championing the talents and building up the self-esteem of each individual employee, the department encouraged managers to send notes to their workers congratulating them on little things, like birthdays or graduations, or to offer expressions of sympathy over a family illness or a difficult personal challenge. While similar displays of kindness certainly occur in non-Japanese organizations, these relationship-building activities are usually systematized in the Japanese company. No one is left out. Birthdays do not escape notice. Important life-cycle events are recognized. And employees are given the sense, paternalistic as it may sound, that the company cares about them, and their families, as unique individuals. At Seiko Instruments, USA, we instituted a similar program which, incidentally, was a product of our suggestion system. As simple and obvious as it sounds, we've had a great deal of positive feedback from employees who appreciate the attention.

In Japan, the first thing a personnel department does is teach new recruits the company's basic business philosophy. These business philosophies are often rooted in Confucianism; new employees pledge to serve society, and to show respect for laws, elders, and community relations. While similar new employee orientations in the United States typically convey a somewhat different set of expectations, new employees in any company benefit greatly from an introduction to the values, not just the procedures, which influence and shape the business organization they have joined. Ideally, these values will include a strong emphasis on social responsibility, which can help employees take additional pride in their work.

In Japan, the new recruits, "freshmen" as they are called, also learn the importance of personal growth, the need to work for the common good, the value of consensus, and the importance of building good human relationships. Often, a "freshman" will sign a "contract" upon joining a company, one that is quite unlike the standard American employment contract. The Japanese employment contract usually states simply that the employee is now a member of the company (not an employee, but a *member*) and that the member pledges to follow the company rules. Ironically, there are frequently no explicit rules stated or written down in this contract. However, there is the implicit assumption of mutual commitment and good will. This is another example of how the Japanese depend not on legal documents, but rather on the feeling of shared responsibility, trust, and mutual commitment.

In a large Japanese company, the incoming freshman class typically spends up to one full year in orientation activities organized by the personnel department, all of which serve to reinforce the new recruits' sense that they work for their company—and not for their boss. In fact, the first identification an employee has is usually with his or her incoming freshman class or group. Often these relationships endure and increase in importance over a period of decades. The esprit within a freshman class of recruits is like the camaraderie experienced by Marines who go through boot camp together.

The Japanese personnel department also introduces young recruits to whatever corporate recreational and vacation facilities might be available. Some Japanese workers, even today, live in company subsidized housing where, occasionally, top managers also reside, in part, to model the appropriate level of commitment to the company.

For example, when my colleague at Toshiba, Mark Tanaka, was promoted to the post of product manager for the company's European group, he moved out of his family home in Ome, outside of Tokyo, and into the company dormitory in Yokohama. He decided to stay in Toshiba's dormitory, Tanaka recalled in a recent letter he wrote to me, because he knew his new job would be tough and he wanted to be "closer to the company headquarters." This dedication to the group is constantly reinforced by the company personnel department, which measures the performance of managers, in large part, in terms of the personal example they set. Tanaka won high marks for his dedication. While it is true that most non-Japanese managers will not be bunking with their charges anytime soon, I do believe managers should be evaluated, preferably by the personnel department, largely on whether their personal example of dedication serves to build morale and a sense of team unity.

The personnel department's responsibility to develop and protect wa extends even to the most mundane of daily routines. When Japanese employees arrive for work in the morning, the personnel department expects each department to reinforce the group orientation by holding a brief daily meeting. Usually, workers stand during these meetings, helping keep them very brief. A pep talk is offered, a group of employees may make a short presentation, and, usually, the company song is sung. The gathering is followed by a short session of calisthenics, in which everyone, from factory workers to top management, participates. Work breaks are rare, and, in order to assure that all hands are on deck at the same time, the lunch hour is rigidly scheduled. The work day is not over, usually, until after the boss leaves. After that, employees feel free to go home. In all cases, the personnel department continually encourages managers to be good role models.

Many Japanese personnel departments are also responsible for organizing their company sports teams, which, once again, usually include, side by side, both top management and production line workers. These sports competitions are very popular. I've even had to reschedule top management meetings because of schedule conflicts arising from visits by our company sports teams from Japan. The entire focus is on building team spirit in the company. Recently, for example, Seiko Instruments Japanese women's running team traveled to the United States to compete against other corporate athletic teams. Prior to their race, Seiko's Japanese runners visited U.S. facilities in northern and southern California, where they helped convey our company's message that Seiko is a competitive and team-oriented business. This traveling athletic team does represent quite an expense but, in reality, it is a wise investment the company has made aimed at fostering a competitive team spirit in the ranks.

Most Japanese companies work very hard to make new employees feel at home. To help with this process, the personnel department usually assigns a senior member of the company to act as a mentor for each new employee. The training for new recruits frequently includes classes in business, philosophy, technical topics, and human relations training related to the company's activities.

For the first 10 or 15 years, Japanese employees all receive basically the same salaries, which are adjusted upward by the personnel department about once a year. Thereafter, modest individual performance-based pay increases are quietly awarded to top performers. During their early years in a company, Japanese employees learn to work with each other, strengthening the bond of loyalty that started with their mutual entry into the company. After about 15 years, these employees will start to compete for their first management job, that of *kacho* (group leader).

The Japanese personnel department plays the central role in all these developments, gluing the company together by enhancing human relationships, developing employee potential, and nurturing in employees the sense that the highest goal they can achieve is to contribute to the efforts of their group (us) against the ever-present competition (them).

Revitalizing the typical non-Japanese personnel department along these lines—providing more training, a more collegial atmosphere, and more tangible and genuine support for the individual employee—is one of the most important structural changes that is within the power of organizational leaders to implement. For this practice to be most effective, of course, it should be done company-wide.

Cross-Training for Everyone

One of the most important functions of the average Japanese personnel department is managing the cross-training of the workforce. The value of this practice is apparent across the range of business activities, from product development to after-sales customer service and support. The benefits of cross-training accrue to both the employee and the company.

In my more than 12 years with Japanese companies, I've seen many of my colleagues change jobs. Since the average Japanese salaryman switches jobs within his company every three to five years, I've seen various people change jobs three or four times since I first met them. The following is a very typical Japanese salaryman career path:

1 year training—including factory work, production, inventory control, and management.

3 years in computer development, engineering.

3 years in application development, engineering.

3 years as application engineer in the domestic market.

2 years studying for MBA in the United States.

3 years in the international sales department.

3 years sales liaison in Europe.

3 years as assistant general manager in the United States.

3 years as kacho (the first management job!) of an international sales department in Tokyo.

3 years as general manager of European sales.

3 years in planning department, Tokyo.

Because these shifts in career paths are the norm, there is no stigma or loss of face when these changes are made. They are not occasions for the territorial battles that erupt when such changes take place in a more static organization. Generally, a person will go from an international assignment back to a domestic one or to a line or staff assignment. The process is also cross-functional; an assignment from sales to operations or to marketing is quite common. For the most part, Japanese male workers usually start out in engineering and then migrate to other areas, like marketing, administration, or customer service. Few return to engineering, due to loss of technical skills, although those skills are occasionally refreshed.

If Japanese businesses enjoy certain advantages over non-Japanese businesses, cross-training is a major reason. Cross-training is a powerful technique because it develops functionally adept middle and senior managers. In addition, it allows managers to move a nonperformer out of a job without any loss of face or fight over territory. We did this at Seiko Instruments, USA, making fairly major job shifts on a regular basis, about every three years, and found that doing so allowed us to easily move performers into various roles with more responsibility and room for growth. At both Toshiba and Seiko Instruments, USA, I've discovered that three years in any one job is, in fact, about the ideal length of service.

When you figure that it takes a year or two to determine if a person is performing in a given job, the three-year time frame is not unduly long. Enough time is allowed to learn and do a job well, but not so much time as to allow a poor performer to permanently cripple an organization. While it means shaking up your ranks, I wholeheartedly endorse this practice of moving people around. Matching the Japanese in this respect will be difficult, but there is simply no reason that Margaret Jones or Bill Smith should be doing the same job for 20 years. Someone else can do their job better. And they can do some other job with a fresh approach and a renewed sense of purpose, as long as the job change is a routine part of the organizational culture.

Indeed, I've often heard complaints from friends and colleagues who tell me they are "burnt out" in some particular job but are reluctant to leave or ask for a reassignment because of a perceived loss of face or loss of power within the company. Such cycles of interest and lack of interest are normal in people and managers should be aware of and capitalize on them. When interest in a job starts to flag, the time is right to switch jobs with someone else who, in all likelihood, is also ready for a change. The benefits of this practice are enormous.

A few non-Japanese organizations already practice some job-switching, but it is not yet the norm outside Japan. I know that before I went to work for Japanese companies every job change I was handed brought with it considerable stress. Was it a promotion? Did I lose face or power in the company? In most non-Japanese companies, it is very hard to make these kinds of changes unless the change is perceived by the reassigned worker as a promotion to a better position with more power.

At Seiko Instruments, USA, I applied the Japanese cross training technique by trying to link all organizational changes to the end of our fiscal year. Personnel changes made in this manner are usually less traumatic and provide a sense of stability even during periods of change. This way, a pattern of organizational evolution replaces crisis management as the officeplace change mechanism. In a static organization, where changes are not routine, every move becomes an ordeal, leading to recriminations, resignations, or rancor. When these changes are expected, the total performance of the company improves. Unlike the average Japanese personnel manager, however, I'm occasionally willing, when appropriate, to make these changes after just one year, rather than wait longer, as is typical in Japan.

Another benefit of cross-training should be obvious. A cross-trained sales account executive, for instance, can impress a potentially important customer, who may have a specialized request, by not offering the standard arms-length lamentation that he'll "have to check with the factory." He already knows, for the most part, what the factory can and cannot do. Ideally, it used to be his job to field those requests when he worked at the factory.

By constantly circulating people from the factory to sales and marketing and then back again, a culture of omniscience is created. To the greatest extent possible, everybody knows everything. In nonmanufacturing industries, like financial institutions or retail outlets, there are still abundant opportunities for job-switching. Wouldn't it be nice if the teller in your bank actually knew at least something about the securities department? Or if the check-out clerk in the grocery store had some idea about when fresh fish is delivered?

One of my Japanese friends tells me that career paths and career development in Japan are a bit like Japanese *miso* soup, a tasty combination of soy beans, salt, small clams, and vegetables. "It has to be stirred up constantly to be any good," he says of the hot liquid that is usually whisked with chopsticks between sips to avoid settling. The more people who are aware of what can and cannot be done, the more likely it is that something worthwhile will happen.

Cross-training is particularly important in international businesses. Most major Japanese companies routinely dispatch people from Japan to their U.S. affiliates for training and development and to facilitate communications, usually on a three-year assignment.

The circulation of talent is not confined to the top tier of these companies. We always have at least one trainee from Seiko Instruments' international sales and marketing department with us in California on a one-year assignment. These trainees, who usually have about five years' experience working in Japan, typically assist the planning manager by working on analyzing purchase orders and sales forecasts.

Seiko Instruments, USA, has refined the practice even further; it currently has a young trainee who works in Japan, not for Seiko Instruments, but for one of the company's suppliers. This junior employee will stay in the United States for about a year, polishing his English and learning more about international marketing and global business. His presence demonstrates not only the importance of cross-training, but also the close, almost family-like relationship between Seiko and its suppliers. Most of my Japanese colleagues have had similar cross-training experiences, going from staff jobs to marketing jobs to line management jobs to engineering jobs and then back again. It is very unusual to find a Seiko Japan employee who has held the same job for more than a few years.

This kind of rotation keeps people challenged and gives them a broad range of experience. Investment in training, of course, assumes there is a high probability that people will stay with the company. And making such an investment turns out to be one good way to keep people engaged. The "I'm not growing in my job anymore" excuse for leaving just does not add up in this kind of environment. The workers *are* constantly growing—and they *are* constantly leaving, albeit to some other place in the company where they can continue to make a contribution.

While the benefits of cross-training accrue most dramatically in larger organizations, my experience tells me this practice is valuable in all companies, regardless of size. Even in a two-person business, it is worthwhile to consider the potential benefits of switching jobs from time to time, when possible, to allow fresh approaches and to prevent organizational stagnation.

Cross-training also has a side benefit of enhancing human relationships within a company and demonstrating a holistic concern for employees. These assignments in various arenas literally bounce people off one another, whom they will bounce off of again and again in other arenas within the company over the years, leading to a more tightly integrated and familiar workforce.

Broad training and experience also provide senior management with a more practical perspective on the company. It becomes possible to understand, with a gut-level feeling, that which can only be learned from direct line experience. Thus, one arm of the business is not left asking another arm if it can do such and such. Instead, the person doing the asking is often able to include a practical suggestion as to just how such and such can be accomplished. This "let me help you with your job" approach cuts both ways, from the engineering side to the marketing side, and back in the other direction.

The key is to get employees accustomed to regular horizontal job moves rather than expecting each move to be up some kind of vertical ladder. For example, in a period of three months Seiko Instruments, USA, made the following horizontal moves in a 200-person organization: a customer engineer became a product marketing specialist; a manufacturing shift supervisor became an operations project manager; a general purpose engineer joined the international marketing group; an operational "floater" became a part of the quality control team; and one engineer, who spent a year with the marketing division, was reassigned back to the research engineering group in which he had previously worked. "I understand my engineering job so much better," the employee told me, "now that I know what our salespeople go through when dealing with customers."

In Japan, facilitating cross-training is the role of the highly empowered personnel department. Frequently the personnel department will maintain a detailed "staffing roadmap" that goes out four or five years. These staffing transition plans are enormously useful. In the product development phase, for example, employees are frequently worried about doing their job so well they might eliminate their position. I know, for example, of one woman in an American company who dragged her feet on installing a new computerized accounting system. She explained to me that once the system was on-line she might be off-line, out of work, and no longer needed. A staffing roadmap in the systems development phase is crucial in that it lets employees know they have a future with the company once they have completed their current assignment. These staffing roadmaps can be a powerful incentive to employees to get on with and finish their current job, especially if they know and look forward to their next destination within the company.

The atmosphere generated by cross-training reaches all the way up and down the organizational chain of command. I was constantly asked, and expected to know, the smallest details of Toshiba's $350 million a year business. It was good discipline for me but it was extremely frustrating at first. Initially, I expected to delegate responsibility for all the small details. But my boss at Toshiba Japan wouldn't let me. And he set the right example by paying incredible attention to every little detail of the computer business, including divisional sales and product inventory levels.

Surprisingly, and most unfortunately, perhaps because it is more difficult and takes more effort, many Japanese employers often do not make the effort to cross-train and rotate non-Japanese employees as they do their linguistically identical Japanese colleagues.

Sadly, I've learned that Westerners who work for Japanese companies, like nearly all the females employed by these firms, are usually considered outsiders regardless of the length of their association with a Japanese company. Clearly, over the long term, this hampers the performance of top non-Japanese managers in Japanese businesses. Instead of increasing their effectiveness as they gain experience and build relationships, Americans employed by Japanese firms commonly find themselves slamming into this hidden wall of insider versus outsider. This problem also exists for female employees of all nationalities in Japanese companies, who typically must endure the most extreme forms of discrimination.

In fact, Western business managers have an awesome and unmatched arsenal of talent in their ranks of well-trained and motivated females. The traditional unequal treatment of women in the Japanese workplace will certainly undermine Japan's competitiveness in the years ahead.

In the past, the unequal treatment of Japan's female workforce did not greatly influence Japan's competitive posture, in part because many non-Japanese corporations seemed content to simply surrender markets to their Japanese competitors. The marketing of the next generation of consumer products, however, ranging from electric cars to high-definition television, promises to create a more competitive environment in which every individual worker, whether male or female, must make a maximum contribution.

As American industry gears up to reenter the consumer electronics industry, for example, Japanese corporations, entirely male-led, will find themselves competing against a larger international talent pool comprised of both men and women. While the Japanese have long neglected and underused female talent in the workplace it is a practice they can no longer afford. And it will be very difficult for most Japanese businesses to make this major and necessary change.

The Japanese language itself is in many ways an obstacle to the full use of the talents of women in Japanese companies. Its rigid and ancient hierarchial structure, for example, requires that women address men in a subordinate verbal posture even when speaking to a lower-ranking male employee. I have had many Japanese females, who are trying to build their careers, tell me they don't like to speak Japanese to Japanese men because it immediately puts them in an inferior position. Japanese women, if they are able, usually prefer to do business in English as there is no need to constantly denigrate themselves in order to communicate.

Japanese companies are usually unwilling to invest in training their female employees. As a result, this highly educated part of their workforce is terribly underused. I've often seen very competent women who have graduated from the top Japanese universities sometimes do little more than serve tea. In the more than 15 years I've been associated with Japanese companies, most of the career moves Japanese women have made are to graduate slowly from tea servers to note takers to, perhaps, administrative assistants.

Management in Japan simply does not consider training and investing in female workers a sound investment. They expect women to leave the workplace at an early age to marry and rear a family as they have traditionally done. If a woman leaves the workforce in Japan when she is 25 years old, it is very difficult for her to return. The Japanese culture and business infrastructure offer no support to women who wish to return to work after having children. While day care is still a problem in many countries, particularly the United States, there are virtually no day care or babysitting centers for children in Japan. Women who do use such services are generally looked down upon. Of course, there are some highly publicized exceptions of women in Japan who have taken strong leadership roles, but attitudes, practices, and institutions work against the effective use of Japanese females in the workforce.

In fact, many common practices in Japan regarding the treatment of female employees have already been banned in most of the West. For example, at Sumitomo Bank, new college graduate female employees are asked to wear the same navy blue corporate uniforms worn by the company's female clerks and secretaries. After two years, female Sumitomo professional employees are finally permitted, like male employees, to select their own attire. "The woman's movement in Japan is going nowhere fast," the *Wall Street Journal* confirmed in a recent front-page article.

This is a major advantage for Western managers. Imagine, if you will, a competition in which one team voluntarily benches half its players. Indeed, many Western companies operating in Japan learned long ago that Japanese women are the best pool of available talent in the country. For example, the American companies that have thrived in Japan, like IBM and Hewlett Packard, freely credit much of their good fortune to their "untraditional," but quite effective, use of Japanese female employees.

Demands for equal treatment in the workplace made by Western women, influenced by the women's liberation movement, are frequently seen by Western businessmen as a nuisance. A necessary, although not always eager, accommodation is often grudgingly enforced by the courts. However, insofar as it concerns the West's economic preparedness, the women's liberation movement has provided an awesome arsenal of human talent that goes virtually untapped by most Japanese businesses. In all probability, it will be generations before Japanese women achieve the hard-won status and opportunities now available to Western women, particularly those in the United States.

The West, on the other hand, is accustomed to seeing women and members of many different ethnic groups in important leadership positions. In America, the old WASP establishment has long since broken apart. The best managers are those who are able to take full advantage of the talents of all people, based on their abilities. By providing cross-training opportunities to all workers, regardless of their sex or outsider status, managers can invite contributions from the entire workforce.

For this reason, western managers can do an even better job of cross-training than now occurs in the typical Japanese company. By applying this powerful technique across the board managers can improve its execution. A cross-trained workforce sets the stage for major company initiatives, ranging from new product development to improved customer service and support. As Wall Street's Michael Blumberg told *Forbes*, "Whenever you have a business that's done the same thing for a long time, a new person can come in and do it better. I guarantee it."

The Japanese Work Ethic versus the Protestant Work Ethic

One of the first things I noticed about my Japanese colleagues is that they are incredibly consistent in their work hours. They are at work by 9:00 A.M., take precisely an hour for lunch, almost always between 12:00 and 1:00, and work hard throughout the duration of the day. There is very little socializing or "hall time."

I remember, for example, inviting one of my Japanese colleagues to go skiing. It is common practice, of course, for Americans to knock off early Friday afternoon to avoid the traffic. When I suggested to him that we do that, he made an awkward excuse. The real reason, I later determined, was that he did not want to leave the office before the official work day was over. Japanese workers, I've learned, expect to give 110% all the time, even including Friday afternoons that may happen to coincide with a ski trip.

This work ethic drives the Japanese manager to lead by example. But unlike the famed Protestant work ethic that helped shape American business, the Japanese work ethic revolves around the group, not the individual. I was always impressed, for example, by how rigorously disciplined my Japanese colleagues took their formal workday and business lunches. What surprised me is that the discipline ends at the office, and the group. Totally devoted to work during the business day, Japanese employees usually take little or no work home with them on weekends or on airplanes. It is an interesting juxtaposition—working intensely when in a group and visible and then resting and relaxing when alone, again demonstrating the group orientation that differentiates the Japanese.

The Japanese work ethic is almost militaristic. Scholars point out that in early Japan, the samurai warrior class was at the top of the feudal structure. Unlike the West, where the military performed at the service of political, religious, or economic institutions, in Japan these institutions were at the service of the samurai, who outranked the merchants and farmers. Even today, Japanese businesses are organized and function according to military tenets. There is always a strong hierarchial structure; there are daily acknowledgments of the differences in rank between individuals; and, in contrast to Western individualism, there is an obsession with loyalty and a deep personal attachment to the group. All of this leads, predictably, to a very strong communal work ethic.

The desire to nurture a strong work ethic is what drives Japanese managers to get their people, whenever possible, working together in groups at the same time in the same place; all hands on the oars simultaneously is the goal of most Japanese managers. Reinforcing the sense of collective identity is easier if everyone shares the same physical space at the same time. Of course, the responsibility to model this behavior, like all others, begins at the top.

In contrast, the Western work ethic is clearly not what it used to be. We have even reached the point where those who work hard and "break a sweat" are often made to feel foolish, as though they were not smart enough to figure out how to get the work done more easily. There is even the popular American saying: "Working hard and working smart are not the same thing." Maybe not. But, given recent cultural predispositions, Western managers do need to constantly address this issue by making it clear that working hard is not the same as not being smart. We must honor our hardest workers and we must recognize effort, not just accomplishment.

Alchemist's Checklist #5
Human Resources Checklist

AMERICAN/WESTERN	JAPANESE
Job is well defined	Job/responsibility is vague
Career paths build skills within a a discipline across many companies	Career paths build skills across many disciplines within one company
Performance evaluations emphasize rational skills	Performance evaluations emphasize effort and sincerity
American management is often hired from the outside, opportunities are always avaliable outside	Japanese managers rise from within the corporate ranks, adding to the feeling of camaraderie and shared experience inside the group

MANAGEMENT TIPS

- Empower your personnel department to act as an employee champion. Have the department take an active role in all performance evaluations and career progressions.

- Regularly recognize the individuality of your employees. Celebrate events: birthdays, graduations, and family milestones.

- Cross-train your people. Create a culture of omniscience.

- Keep stirring the pot. Remember that career paths are like miso soup: It is no good if it settles.

- Encourage and recognize cross-department, and/or cross-function horizontal career moves.

- The perceived behavior of senior management directly affects and establishes your company work ethic.

6

MONEY:

. . . and Other More Subtle Forms of Communication

The Japanese culture offers a treasure trove of subtle communication styles that can dramatically enhance workplace relationships. However, the single biggest communicator in business is money. It cuts across all geographic and cultural boundaries. As Bob Dylan wrote, "Money doesn't talk, it swears." In a business setting, deeds, like who gets paid how much, certainly do speak louder than words. Actions are always the ultimate form of communication.

Whether modeling hard-working behavior by being the first to arrive in the office and the last one to leave, or by working within the line of sight of subordinates, good managers should continually attempt to unify their group. This is particularly difficult in the area of pay and compensation. Indeed, we can work on effective managerial communications until we turn blue and never undo the damage that can be created by that loudest of talkers, money.

In Japan, workers and middle managers receive salaries equivalent to those in America. But Japanese top managers do not command the salaries that most senior American managers enjoy. According to *Newsweek*, the pay differential ratio in Japan between workers and top management is about $1 to $16, while in the United States top managers are paid $100 for every $1 paid to workers. In Germany, managers receive about $25 for every $1 paid to entry-level workers. The German ratio helps show how globally atypical the American practice really is.

The data also demonstrate that Japanese managers and workers operate in an environment that, at a minimum, gives the appearance of being more financially equitable. This sense of workplace equity is very important. Where it is absent, there is a psychological incentive for workers to get even in some way, often by underperforming in their jobs or by dragging their feet, even if this is done without conscious intent.

I've seen many of my Japanese colleagues get visibly upset when we talk about American senior management compensation. They go so far as to say that this high compensation would be considered a social crime in Japan. It is more than out of line, they tell me, it is actually a crime against society!

When Disney's talented executive Michael Eisner received $190 million in compensation in one recent year, a respected financial analyst told the *Los Angeles Times* that, given the company's performance, "he deserved every penny." What about the 58,000 other Disney employees?, I wondered. Do they agree? Could Eisner have done it all on his own? The theory seems to be that if you want to motivate people, you whip the galley slaves. But what do the galley slaves think about this technique? And how do they respond?

It's clear to me that the enormous publicity created by the frequently high rates of executive compensation, particularly at public companies that disclose this information, serve as a huge disincentive to other people in the ranks. These pay rates alone are enough to poison the culture of many companies. Making deals, not products, and cannibalizing rather than building companies is a predictable result of the Western tendency to regard a company as a cash cow executives are allowed to milk to their satisfaction.

The comparison between executive pay rates across countries does, however, overlook at least one important factor: Japanese top managers receive significantly more perks and other special status-enriching benefits than do those who hold comparable positions in American companies. These special benefits, like a company car and driver, access to an executive dining club, or a very generous expense account, signify the symbolic status or power associated with the position. In Japan, symbolic power, insofar as an employee's self-esteem is concerned, is often just as important, or even more so, than the actual cash compensation. In fact, these symbolic perks seem to do a better job of building loyalty from both managers and workers.

The respect granted to senior Japanese managers from employees as a result of visible perks usually leaves them with a greater sense of loyalty to their company than more highly paid non-Japanese executives, who are free to take their stash of cash and quit at any time. Japanese executives who quit lose not only a job, but also a chauffeured car, nights out on the town, and status.

In the American system, the company pays employees and employees buy status symbols. In Japan, the company buys the status symbols for managers, rewarding executives while at the same time reducing apparent salary differentials and reinforcing managers' ties to the company.

At Seiko Instruments, USA, we tested this approach by tying more benefits, such as car allowances, vacation time, and extra health coverage, to seniority. Of course, many Western companies already tie vacation time to seniority, but Seiko Instruments, USA has extended this practice and now applies it to other benefit areas as well. Doing so, we discovered, is one good way to let employees know their long-term service is valued and that special additional compensation is distributed on a fair and equal basis.

Harvard Business School professor Michael Porter is correct, however, when he puts the problem in a broader perspective. Porter theorizes that nations move through three stages. First, they are driven by the natural advantages of their people, geography, and resources. Second, as they advance, they are driven by innovation as they push back the frontiers of technology. Finally, they are driven by their accumulated wealth which, according to Porter, creates "a backward looking, rearguard action to protect what they've got." Porter worries that U.S. businesses may now be in that third, look-over-the-shoulder stage. Unfortunately, the salary structure in many Western companies provides considerable ammunition for Porter's theory. Rather than concentrating on creating more wealth, too many executives, acting in the rearguard mode, often seem primarily concerned with satisfying their own immediate and personal financial goals.

Clearly, it is unlikely the West's top managers will rush out and volunteer to cut their salaries upon hearing this news. However, I've discovered that it is often possible to design compensation packages in ways that better enhance group solidarity and overall corporate performance. For example, expenses that high-level managers usually pick up themselves, like transportation or entertainment costs, can be subsidized more generously by the company in exchange for salary adjustments. The tax implications in the United States may require the company to offset the employee's additional income taxes, but doing so often gives the employer a bigger bang for his or her compensation buck. For example, providing an employee with membership in a country club may, because of group discounts, cost the company less than it would cost the individual. By combining the country club perk with a small raise to cover any tax liability it creates, it is possible to leverage compensation dollars for better results. If the perks are judged by the employee to be meaningful, they can sometimes provide a partial substitute for cash remuneration. At the same time, they also help the employee develop a sense of loyalty to the company that is derived from the high status associated with the provision of what are usually quite visible perks.

In Japan, the most important goal of compensation systems is to develop and nurture a collective identity in an organization. Although it will be difficult and will certainly take some time, American managers must make every effort to bring the salary differentials between workers and managers closer to the Japanese model. In the global economy, it is ultimately counterproductive to tolerate work environments in which the lowest possible worker's wage rates are coupled with very high levels of executive compensation. Over the long term, organizations that practice this inequity are doomed to create ill will in those they need most: the people who actually do most of the work.

Japanese and American employee compensation schemes differ in some other quite important ways. In Japan, salaries are determined by an often complex formula that takes into account many factors. For starters, a base pay level common to all employees working at a common site with an equal number of years of service forms the foundation. Allowances and bonuses are then added to this base pay. The allowances, which consider issues such as the living expenses of the particular employee and transportation costs to get to and from work, can add significantly to the base pay, in some cases as much as $250 to $1,000 monthly.

Worker pay in Japan is also adjusted according to the number of children or dependents in the worker's family. To Westerners, who reason that everyone should get the same money for the same work, this practice may seem unfair. To the Japanese, however, increasing salaries when children are born seems like basic common sense. How, a Japanese executive is apt to reason, will a worker concentrate properly on his job if he can't afford to feed his children? In Japan, the rationale for these pay differences is open, above board, and applicable to all workers, so a sense of fairness is preserved despite the seeming inequality.

Regular and sizable pay bonuses are another mechanism Japanese managers use to tie worker morale to the performance of their company. Most Japanese workers and managers receive bonuses twice a year in amounts that would be considered huge in the West, often totaling four or five months of base salary. These bonuses are based on the performance of the company and their distribution is always a great cause of celebration. This bonus system is very effective because, unlike an equivalent increase in weekly paychecks, the lump sum creates an air of excitement among the employees. It also gives them something to lose, a thought always in the back of their minds. Similar bonuses are now being provided by a handful of American companies, but this motivational technique remains underused in the United States.

Seiko Instruments, USA, currently offers employees the chance to earn a sizable bonus, ranging from 10 to 50% of their base pay. These bonuses, also paid twice a year, are dependent on the performance of their division for junior employees and on the performance of both the division and the total company for more senior managers. Car allowances are based on a combination of need and seniority. Because these bonus programs are carefully structured and well known in the ranks, compensation at Seiko Instruments, USA, is not a black art. Everyone knows exactly what they have to do to earn meaningful financial rewards.

Like bonuses, pay raises in Japan usually serve to unite rather than divide organizations. Rather than just give raises to star performers, the Japanese personnel evaluation system places a far greater emphasis on maintaining a sense of fairness and equity. Production employees may get a raise to compensate them for particularly harsh conditions, such as working in an building without air-conditioning or in an especially noisy or risky environment. In Japan, managers qualify for raises depending on how well they have maintained harmony within their group, respected the established processes in the company, and if their employees report that they have been sincere, honest, and dedicated.

The very top Japanese managers are, of course, also evaluated in terms of more conventional criteria like increased sales, volume of output, and the like, but the heavy emphasis when determining appropriate pay raises in Japan is always on the process issues related to company harmony, individual personality traits, and future potential.

To properly motivate, to communicate the right message to employees, bonuses and pay raises, based on more egalitarian criteria, must be offered across the board in the United States as they are in Japan, as is done at Seiko Instruments, USA. Establishing group achievement goals, for example, offers the opportunity to provide meaningful financial group merit awards as well. You simply have to prove, with dollars, that if a company does well the employees, all of them, will also do well. Perks and other status-enhancing bonuses, like full medical co-payment coverage, can compensate, in part, for lower executive salaries as can stock incentives and equity buy-in plans.

While this change will not come easily, it will come. In fact, marketplace dynamics will likely take care of those companies that fail to make this change, in many cases putting them out of business entirely. Many of America's Fortune 500 companies, for example, which as a group have cut more jobs than they have created in the past decade, have such insecure futures they are frequently likened to dinosaurs.

In the end, the best compensation for leveling the salary range, increasing the distribution of bonus payments, and assuring the fairness of pay raises is the creation of structurally solid and unified organizations. The organizations that make this change will endure and thrive while those that don't probably won't. When workers are compensated fairly they know they are on the same team with management and together they can work like tigers—or even better, hungry tigers.

Open and Continuous Communication

After the screaming importance of money and salary structures is appreciated, it becomes possible to address some of the more subtle forms of communication within an organization. Again, these patterns are quite different in Japan and in the West. For example, I have a Japanese friend at Nippon Steel who once explained to me why he thought, aside from the differences in physical stature, American football would never catch on in the Land of the Rising Sun.

"In the huddle," he said, "only the quarterback talks. In a Japanese huddle, everyone would have to talk." He was only half-joking.

The amount of communication in an average Japanese company cannot be overstated. At Toshiba, I once analyzed the amount of time I spent on sideways, or dotted line, communications, that is, face-to-face discussions with colleagues and associates other than subordinates or supervisors. It amounted to over 60 hours per month, about 30% of my time. This would be unheard of in a typical American company.

Whenever an important item came up at Toshiba, for example, I was expected to personally communicate the information to the president of the American subsidiary, the general manager of the American subsidiary, the senior manager of the international sales and marketing group in Japan, the general manager of the international sales and marketing group in Japan, and the general manager of the computer division factory. A memo simply would not do.

Each of these individuals would want to hear, in excruciating detail, what was going on. They would then talk among themselves to further sharpen their understanding of the subject. While some of this was due to the desire to avoid misunderstandings arising out of the fact that I am an English-speaking American, this huge amount of verbal communication is routine among Japanese managers and workers. Some scholars point, rightly I believe, to the awkward and difficult Japanese written language as being largely responsible for this highly charged pattern of verbal interaction. Given the difficulty of writing in Japanese, it is much easier, even though time-consuming, to communicate with the spoken word. Non-Japanese, of course, are not burdened with this linguistic constraint. Nonetheless, bringing the amount of personal workplace communication closer to the level found in most Japanese companies offers some powerful advantages.

Indeed, the importance of worker/management communications has received considerable attention in recent years, as evidenced by the now-popular "management by walking around" school. However, in most non-Japanese settings a manager who spends 30% of his or her time "just talking" with associates, as I did at Toshiba, is still liable to be disciplined or branded a busybody. Japanese managers, on the other hand, are required to be constantly engaged in a process of open and continuous communication with colleagues.

This open communication takes place throughout the business day, facilitated in part by the Japanese custom of open offices. When you go into a Japanese office, you usually find a completely open work space grouped by departments. Although it certainly is noisy, the setting does foster communication. Since most Japanese workers look at their company as a place to learn, not just work, the open office serves as a kind of classroom in which workers and bosses become familiar with each other's assignments and routines.

"I hated the idea at first," Jeffrey Smith, longtime executive in Toyota's United States Motor Sales Division says. When Toyota decided to set up its huge office in Kentucky, Smith helped select the site. "I showed them the floor plan, with six-foot partitions and such, and explained that we needed more space." Smith recalls that his Japanese colleagues laughed. "But Mr. Sato is only five feet, three inches tall. How will he see over the partition?" they asked.

Smith's Japanese superiors quickly sketched out an alternative scheme. They removed the partitions, pushed the desks closer together, and placed the department heads' desks in direct line of sight with the rest of the group, thereby quadrupling the number of employees in the same office space.

"I'm convinced this is the most effective way to organize an office," Smith now says. Interestingly, the only organizations in the West that routinely use this kind of open office layout are journalistic newsrooms, police departments, trading houses, and military command centers. The assumption these organizations make is that events will require an immediate marshaling of forces for an appropriate response—a major stock market move, a breaking news story, a dire community emergency, or a charge on the battlefield. Japanese managers tend to look at all business activities this way; a premium is placed on constant and immediate communication because sudden events, problems, and opportunities are always anticipated. In these settings, surprises are expected.

The typical Japanese office layout is especially useful for freshman or junior members of the group who can learn many things by observing senior group members' daily activities. At the same time, the manager, whose desk is usually found at the front of the undivided room, can, just like a school teacher, observe how his or her group is working and get a rough idea of each member's progress. Informally, in this setting, it becomes possible to help workers improve without giving them special training seminars outside the office.

The Japanese office layout, consisting of desks and no cubicles (even for the senior manager), is designed to facilitate open communication, albeit at the expense of privacy, quietness, and "thinking space." This arrangement, commonplace in Japan, is resisted strongly by most Western workers. However, many successful Western companies, like the M&M Mars corporation, have employed this scheme for years.

At Seiko Instruments, USA, our operations department recently had to retreat temporarily from their office cubicles to an open space arrangement during a two-month office reconstruction period. There was quite a lot of grumbling at first, as employees complained that they felt naked and exposed in this setting. However, after some time, most of the employees said they liked to see and hear what other people were doing. Eventually, we found a good middle ground between the Western and Japanese styles, redesigning the office using relatively low four-foot partitions for almost all of the offices, including middle-level managers. We did retain some private offices for the most senior managers, since they often have visitors and their offices are sometimes seen as a symbol of the company. However, I personally modeled the appropriate behavior by always keeping my door wide open except in the most unusual situation.

The lesson seems clear: Private offices are counterproductive if they get in the way of open and continuous communication. At a minimum, office doors should be kept open and a culture of constant interaction should be encouraged. Glass offices, gaining popularity in Japan, are another option. The goal is to turn the office into more than an office. It should also be a learning center where each employee can make daily gains by observing and emulating successful co-workers and managers.

Most businesses would benefit from erring on the side of more openness in their office settings. While it may occasionally be necessary to retreat into private offices in some sensitive occupations or at particular moments, once the private office setting becomes routine people rarely emerge from their cloistered shelters. It will take some getting used to, but open offices provide a more dynamic setting that can improve productivity and enhance group solidarity.

Contextual Communication

One of the most interesting areas of communications research concerns the degree to which the context of a communication overshadows and influences whatever specific messages are being communicated. Marshall McLuan's famous observation that "the medium is the message" has important implications for business communications even when no medium per se is involved. Specifically, I've noticed how wildly different the atmospherics are when it comes to communicating messages from one party to another in Japan and in the West.

Japan is a very high-context culture. Context refers to how much one can assume others already know about the subject under discussion. In low-context communications, the listener knows very little and so must be told practically everything. In high-context communications, the listener is already pretty much up to speed and, consequently, can skip over the informational stages of a conversation, moving quickly into careful analysis of the information at hand.

Most Americans and Northern Europeans operate in a very low-context environment. For example, a top Western executive working in his office typically receives his normal quota of visitors one at a time. Most of the information relevant to the executive's job originates with the few people he sees regularly in the course of an average day. This is why the advisors who surround a Western executive are so important; they have his ear and can be his only, or at the least, his major, link with the world outside his walled-off office. They alone control the content and the flow of information to the boss.

The offices of top Japanese businesspersons, vice presidents, and the most senior managers, in contrast, are usually shared offices. This is not done to save money on office space, as some may think, although that is another small side benefit. This arrangement helps people share information more effectively; it creates an atmosphere of high-context communication. People are constantly coming and going from these shared executive offices and practically everyone knows what is going on at all moments.

Usually, these open executive offices include a space designed for meeting guests. A sofa, two easy chairs, and a coffee table strategically set off from the rest of the room by a lamp stand or room divider create the psychological sense of a separate area that remains, nonetheless, within earshot of everyone. In Japan, the function of a company's leadership is centered on gathering, processing, and disseminating information. In this high-context environment, everybody stays informed about every aspect of the business.

Establishing effective managerial communication means paying at least some attention to these issues. The settings in which workplace discussions take place influence the nature of those interactions. The best managers are those who move away from the remote, low-context, "let me tell you what to do" approach to a more high-context, collaborative, and inclusive communication style. This technique, of course, requires a steady diet of person-to-person exchanges.

The West has the advantage of being able to make better use of the written word to help accomplish this goal. English, like most non-Asian languages, has a relatively more simple alphabet and structure. For this reason, Westerners tend to make much better and more widespread use of new personal computer-based communication tools, such as electronic mail, which, for linguistic reasons, are not very popular in Japan and probably never will be. By combining the traditional Japanese attention to physical issues, like open office environments, with the now common Western use of personal computer communication technologies, managers can elevate business interactions to a more effective high-context level.

Call Me Bill

People in the West tend to substitute first-name familiarity for a more genuine pattern of effective interpersonal communication. It is easy to tell a subordinate to call you by your first name; it is much harder to make the more laborious and time-consuming effort required to create a solid and mutually recognized context within which understanding and communication can really be achieved. I, for one, was quite surprised to learn that effective business communications do not require and can even be hampered by first-name familiarity. The Japanese culture, which emphasizes titles and family names, had a very big influence on this realization.

I recall, for example, my very first trip to Japan, in 1976, when I made some sales calls with a new colleague, Mr. Takamatsu, who worked for our agent, Overseas Data Services. The first thing I did was ask Mr. Takamatsu the names of the other people who would be accompanying us on the sales calls. He told me a Mr. Kobayashi would be joining us so I asked Mr. Takamatsu for Mr. Kobayashi's first name. Mr. Takamatsu looked puzzled. Finally, he shrugged and told me that, although he had worked with Mr. Kobayashi for nearly 15 years, he had no idea what his first name was!

This episode was one of the first indications that I was operating in a very different culture. Later, I came to understand that the formal manner whereby Japanese address one another with last names only is yet another manifestation of the culturally mandated practice of identifying with the group, in this case, the family name, rather than the individual. This formal distance in salutations, however, masks the intensive and deep high-context communication that is a constant and overriding feature of the typical Japanese business organization.

With the exception of their reluctance to use written and E-Mail communications, the Japanese are unusually sophisticated when it comes to interpersonal communication. The very complex written characters used in the Japanese language help account for this. Given the difficulty of communicating in written Japanese, even for the Japanese themselves, most Japanese find it much easier to talk with a colleague than to write a memo or send an E-Mail message. The result is quite a lot of face-to-face meetings in which Japanese talk over matters that most non-Japanese might convey in writing.

Effective communication is, of course, a key to efficient management and most Japanese managers seem to know instinctively that it is not the message that matters, but how that message is massaged, how it is presented, that helps determine whether communication, in fact, actually takes place.

For example, anyone who has ever watched a group of Japanese engage in heated conversation immediately notices some strange and different practices. Most noticeably, when one Japanese speaks there is a constant and reinforcing patter that emanates from the person listening. The Japanese call this *aizuchi*, which means, literally, "to chime in with."

This practice, reflexive and habitual, assures the speaker that the listener is tuned in and following along. English speakers, even with their occasional "uh-huhs" and "I sees," do not come close to mimicking the more finely honed Japanese practice of listening proactively and simultaneously confirming receipt of the message, usually with the words *Hi* (yes), or *Ahso deska*? (is that so?), or simply *Ahso*.

In fact, the highly stylized and hierarchical Japanese language provides a verbal structure that, like the written language, differs from English in many ways. While the Japanese workplace does appear to be more egalitarian than its Western counterpart, the spoken Japanese language helps counterbalance this fact.

In Japanese, there are many specific words, phrases, and tones that a manager utilizes when speaking to a subordinate. Quite different status-determined linguistic honorifics are used when that employee talks to or about the boss. This rigid recognition of rank and adherence to verbal honorifics are expected in the Japanese work setting.

In America, in contrast, there is often an informal collegiality in the office, represented by the "call me Bill" kind of CEO. He wanders around telling everyone from the receptionist to the janitor to "call me Bill." That's fine. Nothing wrong with that. The problem, however, is that too often "Bill" thinks his responsibility to interact with lower-ranking employees is satisfied once he has done them the honor of putting them on a first-name basis with him. So Bill doesn't ask the receptionist if the new phone system is working and doesn't ask the janitor's impression of how the company might reduce its waste expenses, questions that would be on top of the list for a more formal Japanese manager.

The typical Japanese executive is much less interested in generating the "call me Yoshi" kind of Western informality. In fact, I know many Japanese colleagues who, like Mr. Takamatsu and Mr. Kobayashi, have worked together for decades and still address one another by their honorific titles.

In place of the superficial approval characterized by the American practice of calling virtual strangers by their first names, which the Japanese find rather odd, most Japanese managers seek instead to cultivate a climate of total communication. The typical boss who tells her employees to call her by her first name often knows much less about what these employees really think than does the more seemingly remote Japanese boss.

The Japanese language, with its strict rules about rank and status, provides a sense of structure and order in the office. With the ranking order clear and always in place, the group is then able to pull together in common pursuits, sharing information and developing and then implementing strategies. No one is left feeling they are receiving inadequate respect from their colleagues.

On the other hand, old "call me Bill" is sometimes so insecure about his status within the company that his insecurity interferes with harmonious group performance. For instance, in a superficially informal setting one often finds the "executive sessions," or the top-down, we'll-tell-you-what-we-decide management by fiat approach.

The Japanese language, by contrast, affords different opportunities. Because Japanese managers, at every turn, are being verbally honored for their status, much the way U.S. senators are on the floor of the Senate, they are confident and secure in their status and do not feel the need to throw their weight around in order to prove they are in charge. The overriding air of mutual respect created by formally addressing colleagues somehow creates a climate in which deeper communication can take place.

Non-Japanese bosses sometimes seek the same status the Japanese derive from their respectful salutations by calling the shots and asserting authority. In the end, however, it is much more effective to have people call you "Mr. Williams" and then ask them what they think, rather than be called "Bill" and run around telling everyone what to do. Status is an important consideration, motivating people at work and in their personal pursuits.

Like many of the dichotomies between typical American and Japanese practices, a middle ground can be found between the two approaches. While it is important to understand the role the rigid rank-conscious Japanese language plays in creating clear organizational roles, such rigidity may be counterproductive in American businesses. Combining American-style superficial informality with the Japanese quest for deep communication is the best solution.

To do this, managers must escape the trap of thinking that putting their employees on a first-name basis is the be-all and end-all of effective management communication. The Japanese I've worked with have shown me that being on a first-name basis and communicating efficiently are not the same thing.

At Seiko Instruments, USA, I made a significant commitment to communicating with employees. I personally sit down with hundreds of employees each year, carefully going over the company's business plans and soliciting their ideas. In addition, I am always quite open about our performance. Every six months we post a report card of what we have accomplished, financially and nonfinancially, and what we hope to accomplish in the next six months. I also attend our monthly "Brown Bag University" sessions, where training and motivation are provided to small groups of workers and managers. My presence helps emphasize the importance of the training and provides another opportunity to interact with all levels and divisions in our company.

I also encourage my employees and managers to make regular use of E-Mail. E-Mail is a major communications advantage enjoyed by English speakers, who are more comfortable with their written language, on average, than are most Japanese. In the West, E-Mail is an excellent way to emulate the Japanese emphasis on interpersonal communications without consuming too much time. The use of E-Mail can help communication-minded Western managers outhustle most Japanese managers in the communications game.

Managers should also conduct regular staff meetings, preferably on at least a weekly basis. Usually an hour or so on Monday mornings is best. From time to time, I offer my managers a training session on how to conduct these meetings. Start on time, begin by announcing the topic and the time the meeting will end, and solicit comments from as many participants as possible. Communication is greatly enhanced if employees know there is a regular opportunity to find out what is going on and to offer their views about work issues.

I write a long column in the quarterly company newsletter in which I am very frank about what is going on in the organization. I also make a point of walking over to somebody's office, rather than sending a memo, whenever possible. In addition to walking off a few calories, this gives me another chance to see and be seen. Face-to-face discussions invariably produce more back-and-forth communication than does a written document. I am certainly comfortable with workers calling me by my first name, but I do not let the familiarity end there.

Strategic Silence

Communication in business requires more than talking. Listening, and hearing what is really being said, are also vitally important. Anyone who goes through a business meeting with Japanese colleagues will immediately notice a phenomenon I found most unsettling at first: long—sometimes very long—periods of silence.

Most Japanese I've encountered seem to know instinctively how to use silence to enhance communication. The usual non-Japanese response is to squirm awkwardly and attempt to fill the void with banter of some kind. The more a non-Japanese person talks, however, the quieter a Japanese person usually becomes. Only after the other person has finished speaking, up to a full minute later, will the Japanese open up with a response or reaction. When I've asked about this practice, I've been informed that my Japanese colleagues want to enhance the dialogue by not missing a single thing the other person might want to say, both verbally and non-verbally.

This approach is quite different from the usual Western business meeting. A recent study conducted at the University of Southern California, for instance, revealed that Americans could typically tolerate just 12 to 15 seconds of silence in a business meeting. For the Japanese, the researchers found that silent periods four times that length were common.

This has important implications for both negotiations and personnel management. For example, while a Western boss might call an underperforming subordinate into his office and berate or even yell at him, a displeased Japanese boss is more likely to use the silent treatment. He will open the meeting by asking the employee a question like, "What accounts for the problems you're having?" He will then listen to the answer. And when the response is complete, the boss will keep listening—and keep listening until the squirming that results generates more meaningful answers.

The Japanese even have a phrase, *Bushi ni go wa nai*, which translates as "a samurai has no second word." Silence is used not to intimidate an employee, but to take the time required to solicit and develop strategies for fixing whatever problem has emerged. I've tested this approach by forcing myself to remain silent, even when it is uncomfortable to do so, and have found that it often does elicit important comments or observations from employees who otherwise would not have talked.

Most Japanese executives I've worked with are simply not interested in hearing excuses. "Bushi ni go wa nai," they'll say, which means, in essence, "Tell me how you are going to fix the problem and meet the original commitment you made." I constantly challenge my general managers and sales managers with this approach. I tell them of the expectations held of the samurai, that it is their responsibility to come up with countermeasures to budget variances in order to meet the original commitments they have made, rather than be articulate brokers of the reasons why such performance is impossible.

The silence that follows a worker's apology for some performance deficit is never a form of punishment, although it may feel that way. Instead, it represents an opportunity for the employee to redeem himself or herself through some act of genuine contrition. In Japan, when the boss is silent, employees are expected to make a sincere apology, once, and not offer any excuses. They are also expected to explain what they have learned from the episode.

The best Japanese managers I've worked with can be very forgiving, but rarely in the absence of a sincere apology. The typical Japanese boss will usually wait, in silence, for as long at it takes for a heartfelt apology. Although it will take some practice, non-Japanese managers should experiment with this form of silent communication. No criticism is more effective or more redemptive than sincere self-criticism. In silence, this self-criticism can emerge. However, if an employee is being verbally attacked, the need for mounting a point-by-point defense can divert attention from under-standing and overcoming the problem.

For example, there is a senior manager at Seiko Instruments, USA, who customarily began most of our early meetings with a long list of excuses even though there clearly was room for improvement. Eventually, I simply cut him off with a polite request that he be quiet. After a few minutes of contemplation I asked him what he was going to do to improve the situation. I then listened carefully. When his answer was not to my satisfaction, I waited until he was clearly finished and then asked the same question, in the same tone, again. Another period of silence followed his answer. By the time we hit the third silent period I finally started getting past the excuses, past the defensiveness, and to the improvement strategies that were required by the situation. It took a combination of patience and silence before any real communication took place.

Linguists agree that, across cultures, up to 70% of all communication takes place nonverbally, through body language, eye contact, and facial expressions. The Japanese seem much more consciously aware of the importance of these nonverbal communications than are most English-speakers. Silence, of course, provides an ideal forum for nonverbal communication.

Silent periods are also valuable in group settings because they enable participants to fully state their views. If, as often occurs, you have one or two people dominating a conversation it can be difficult for others to get a word in. But if you have people talking and then lots of silence, an opening is created for those who might otherwise feel intimidated. This style of proactive listening is a powerful glue in the communication process.

In Japan, the patient listener is a respected figure. At Seiko Instruments, USA, I tried to model this listening behavior in all company meetings. My goal was to achieve a balance between silence and noise and, when necessary, I spent time restraining our more talkative workers. Privately, I asked them to spend more time listening.

One good technique is to force yourself to silently count to five, slowly, after you think a colleague is finished speaking. If that person starts to talk again during this interval period, wait another five-count after he or she has finished. Talk only when the silence booms in your ears. To most Westerners, this exercise feels awkward at first. With practice, it becomes clear how much more communication actually takes place when differing levels of verbosity are accommodated.

By giving colleagues, associates, and employees your ear, and by making it plain that you are as interested in hearing as you are in talking, the lines of communication are kept open. A manager's job is to keep those communication conduits functioning. Listening carefully, and often, is the best technique to make that happen. Remember this simple rule: "The first person to speak, loses!" Listen, listen, listen.

Deliberate Ambiguity

In Japan, the mechanics of interpersonal communication go way beyond the realization that there are outer layers of truth (tatemae) and inner truths (honne). Of course, the importance and influence of vital tangible factors, such as salary structures or office environments, cannot be overlooked. However, there is also a variety of very subtle nuances at work when any boss and employee communicate. I've learned that one of the most important of these nuances is the way precision can sometimes be an enemy of clarity.

For example, I recall seeing a report in the *Wall Street Journal* about an American businessman complaining about dealing with Japanese officials. He told about being bewildered by a jumble of ambiguous guidelines. "I discovered rules with different names," he moaned. "There were 'verbal instructions,' 'suggestions,' 'advices,' 'internal rules,' and 'industry association guidelines.'" He suggested the tangle appeared to be designed to frustrate outsiders and cause them to give up and go home. Maybe so.

However, the Japanese are often just as ambiguous with one another as they are with outsiders. Just as the Japanese seem to have perfected the use of silence in a conversation, so too they have elevated the use of ambiguity to a high art form.

There is a certain power in vagueness. Many companies, particularly those stuck in a traditional mode, are famous for practicing SOP (standard operating procedures). These companies still have SOP books in which each job slot or task is listed and routinized. Precise instructions are provided to the employee, down to, in many instances, the most remarkable levels of detail.

Japanese managers, on the other hand, rarely provide that kind of detailed instruction, particularly to white-collar or sales employees. While workers will no doubt be told how their predecessors did a certain job, the expectation is that employees will find the best way they can do the job. Thus, a Western boss might tell an employee, "I want you to do 'A,' 'B,' and then 'C,'" while a Japanese manager is more likely to say "A to C needs to be done and I want you to do your best."

That way, the employee has a free hand to do things better than did her or his predecessor, and to go on and do D, E, F, G, H, and so on, on the road to "doing their best." The precise instructions provided by many Western managers reflect what has been called a "pacesetting" management style. The pacesetting manager tells workers what to do and how to do it, then urges them to do it faster and better.

In Japan, there are fewer pacesetters and more "coaches," managers who seek to support their workers as if they are athletes. Like athletes, most workers are fully capable of out-performing their coaches, so the role of the coach is not to tell them exactly what to do, but rather to offer support, experience, and encouragement.

Using this strategy, workers are told what needs to be done and not what they specifically should do. Managers then stand back, offer support, and frequently find themselves basking in what is always the ultimate reward for any competent supervisor: The employee who surprises everyone by improving a process from the bottom up or doing what others thought could not be done.

Sometimes my best managers tell me they worry about giving ambiguous instructions. They fear that a lack of precision might allow their subordinates to do less than the situation requires. My Japanese colleagues, culturally predisposed to expect more from each other, see in ambiguity an opportunity to get more than might be expected. To enjoy the benefits of ambiguity a manager must first succeed in creating a cohesive and unified group. If that is accomplished, then an ambiguous leadership style can urge individuals on to moments of greatness that could never have been demanded, predicted, or expected.

Alchemist's Tool Kit #6
Communication Matters Checklist

AMERICAN/WESTERN	JAPANESE
Large salary difference between senior management and workers	Reasonable salary difference between senior management and workers
Communications: generally one way	Communications: interactive/open
Clarity of expression	Ambiguity
Say what you mean	Contextual; vague
Open; respond quickly	Reveal self slowly; respond after thought
Low-context communications, need information	Higher-context communications, already have information
Verbal: uncomfortable with silence	Often nonverbal: silent

MANAGEMENT TIPS

- Money talks: design performance-based compensation schemes that unite rather than divide management and workers.

- Compensate senior management with perks that tie them to the company rather than highly visible, excessive cash compensation packages.

- If the workers are suffering with layoffs or major bonus cuts, then senior management must suffer alongside them with visible pay cuts.

- Create a work environment that encourages open and continuous communication, like the office layout environment in newsrooms, brokerage houses, police departments, and most Japanese companies.

- Develop high-context communication in your organization by encouraging the constant sharing of information.

- Active and ongoing interpersonal communication is necessary for successful group performance over time. Make a serious and consistent commitment to improving vertical and horizontal communication.

- Try to make your office layout and environment an open learning center for all employees.

- Use effective, on-time and well-framed meetings with clear objectives as part of improving communication.

- Don't be a "Bill." First names are fine, but do not substitute superficial informality for meaningful interactions.

- Use strategic silence to enhance communication. Remember, the first person to speak loses!

- Understand that 70% of interpersonal communication is nonverbal. Allow for this nonverbal communication by letting silence take place.

- During meetings, show just as much respect and recognition for listeners as you do for the "noisy" people.

- Use silence in the performance review process to allow the reviewee to feel comfortable to respond to criticism or praise.

- Be aware of the utility of ambiguity, but be ready and able to give a firm "yes" or "no" when required.

7

AGGRESSIVE PATIENCE:

The Alchemy of Decision-Making

Making a decision is a manager's most visible action. Workers may be unaware of many managerial activities, but real-life decisions made by managers usually reverberate rapidly through a workplace. In addition to giving day-to-day direction to a company or division, decisions also provide important insights into the overall character of those making them. They help define company philosophies and shape not only the business strategies of a company, but its culture as well.

As in other areas, there are some rather profound differences between the Western-style decision-making process and the one more typically found in Japan. Different business decision-making approaches, of course, have their own strengths and weaknesses. The trick is in recognizing these differences and knowing when it may be more useful to favor one technique over another.

In general, Westerners are very good at making fast decisions under pressure. Japanese managers, on the other hand, excel at making decisions, albeit in a slower fashion, which are regarded not as executive dictates, but as carefully considered group commitments.

In his book, *Hidden Differences,* Japan scholar Edward Hall illustrates this point by recounting a story he heard from a professor at the University of Kyoto. The Japanese, Hall relates, have a famous saying: "When the wind blows, it is a good time for the makers of wooden tubs." This aphorism exemplifies, better than anything else, the process of *okeya ronri,* a form of circular logic used in the Japanese decision-making process.

Now, one might ask, why is the wind good for the makers of wooden tubs? Well, try this exercise in Japanese circular logic on for size: When the wind blows, it kicks up dust and sand and makes people uncomfortable and depressed. To overcome their depression, they play a stringed instrument called the *shamisen,* whose strings are made out of cat gut. Therefore people kill cats in order to string their shamisens, and the reduction in the number of cats soon leads to an increase in the number of mice. The mice, in turn, gnaw the wooden tubs in which grain is stored, which increases the demand for wooden grain-storage tubs. Hence, "when the wind blows, it is good for makers of wooden tubs." This phrase is often used in Japanese business settings to point out the potential for unintended consequences.

This apocryphal story may seem far-fetched to most Westerners but it does express the Japanese preoccupation with looking at all possible long-term implications of any decision, from a variety of viewpoints, as well as the relationship between seemingly unrelated systems and procedures. As one Japanese colleague once said, "You Americans deal with islands of information; we Japanese deal with the sea of information."

The Japanese executives I've worked with do tend to take more time and dig more deeply than most Westerners for the information they need to make a decision; they usually do not shoot from the hip—even, unfortunately, when a quick shot might be required in a given situation.

Nonetheless, there are some advantages to the Japanese decision-making approach in certain circumstances. More specifically, my experience with Japanese companies has taught me that *how* I make a decision can be even more important than whatever decision I eventually make.

Aggressive Patience

At a recent symposium designed to assist Americans in their business dealings with Japanese, I heard one complaint voiced repeatedly: "Our Japanese partners keep asking the same questions over and over again," moaned one frustrated American after another. "Sometimes the same person asks the same question they asked last week. Sometimes a different member of the team asks a question we thought we answered months ago. The questions, the same questions, keep coming back at us over and over and over again." The Americans wondered if the Japanese were playing some kind of game, stalling for time or setting them up for some later insidious power play.

I've often felt the same frustration with my Japanese colleagues but, like so many learning opportunities that start out looking like brick walls, I've learned there can be a subtle but enormous power in what sometimes appears to be the innate Japanese inability to make a decision. In fact, the consensus management style that acts like stickum holding the typical Japanese team together is most apparent in the interpersonal mechanics of the Japanese decision-making process.

In Japan, in most instances, a business activity is undertaken only after total commitment from the group affected is solicited, nurtured, and formalized. Employing this management style takes a combination of patience and aggressiveness, or, if you will, aggressive patience.

The importance of aggressive patience has been driven home to me over and over again. Shortly after taking over as president of Seiko Instruments, USA, for example, I found myself in something of a quandary. I had been with the company for about a year and a half and our ColorGraphics Peripherals division had finally attained profitability and started hitting its budget targets. However, I knew we still had a tough fight on our hands; our products had to be more carefully focused and more resources were needed for global marketing and advanced product development.

The company's leaders in Tokyo at first appeared to turn a deaf ear to my requests. At every subsequent opportunity, in presentations I made to many different levels of management, I patiently reiterated my plea, seeking support for my business development plans. After approximately nine months, my Japanese colleagues started to respond. Eventually, one explained the delay: "We wondered why you were making these requests so we ignored your message in the beginning, but your message is consistent and you are personally doing what you said needs to be done so we're starting to believe you." This is an example of aggressive patience. Sometimes it just takes time for a message to sink in.

While waiting for a positive response to emerge from Seiko Instrument's top management I worked at never displaying my frustration, although I was certainly quite frustrated at times. More important, I never gave up. I never took the attitude that, well, I've told them what needs to be done so I'm off the hook. Too often, I've heard a manager try to explain away a blunder or missed opportunity with the excuse that he or she "recommended" a different course of action at the time. That is never enough. If you know you are right then you simply must stick to your guns.

As a manager, I've found it useful to impart this aggressive patience technique to all employees. Oftentimes, a good new idea can quickly evaporate into thin air if not implemented immediately. And usually, good ideas run into the barrier of organizational inertia, even in the most dynamic settings. The solution is to make sure the owner of the idea understands and exercises aggressive patience. A good manager should make it clear to workers that they have not met their responsibilities by merely suggesting an appropriate course of action. The job is not done until all affected parties have signed on to the solution.

In certain situations, of course, it might be impossible to achieve this kind of consensus. Sometimes, when faced with a crisis of some sort, a manager must take decisive action even in the absence of such agreement. In these instances, the Japanese preference for consensus largely accounts for their notoriously slow response to sudden business developments. As I've learned, Japanese businesses are like ocean liners: It usually takes a painfully long time to change direction.

In fact, the average non-Japanese manager has an enormous advantage over Japanese competitors when it comes to dealing with crisis situations or sudden opportunities. In addition to emphasizing ambiguity, the process of consensus decision-making in Japan does not train or encourage individual leadership or gutsy, risk-taking behavior. Most of the Japanese managers I've known have such a great fear of making mistakes they often study a problem to death trying to gain consensus among an often huge constituency prior to taking any potentially risky individual action.

Most Western managers are far better than average Japanese managers at seizing the moment and taking advantage of sudden developments. Meeting challenges quickly, fully, and head-on is a signature Western management trait. In a crisis situation, there is simply no time for the elaborate consensus-building preferred by the Japanese. Similarly, when presented with a sudden opportunity that requires a fast decision many Japanese organizations find themselves stuck in an organizational limbo, unable to reach a decision until well after the moment of opportunity has passed.

Toshiba clearly suffered when it was revealed that a Toshiba subsidiary had violated technology control export rules by selling restricted military parts to the former Soviet Union. At the time, there was no clear Toshiba leader in the United States empowered to make a decision and speak for the company. No one could even offer an apology. Every decision had to go back to the committee stationed in Tokyo, which had to gain consensus before acting.

In most crisis situations, a prompt response is crucial. It is usually best to come clean right away. Even if mistakes are made on details, management is demonstrating that it cares about the problem and is attempting to take corrective action, which can then be modified as needed. In the West, not responding to a crisis or to a sudden opportunity in a timely manner may be misconstrued as a lack of interest or, even worse, incompetence.

The Western ability to respond quickly to a crisis or to take advantage of a sudden opportunity is a key ingredient for overall managerial success that most Japanese managers are unable to match. Distinguishing between these crisis situations, which require fast action, and more routine decisions, which do not, is a key managerial responsibility. In general terms, a crisis situation is one in which making an incomplete or even bad decision is clearly worse than making no decision at all. A noncrisis situation, in contrast, is one in which postponing a decision creates few, or at least tolerable, problems.

When time and circumstances allow it, building consensus in the ranks is well worth the effort. Doing so requires a combination of patience and aggressiveness.

Mutual Surveillance

Former Harvard professor Tom Lifson, who speaks fluent Japanese and conducts excellent seminars on doing business in Japan, points out that the very concept of work itself differs in Japan and in the West. This accounts, in part, for the very different decision-making styles in both countries. According to Lifson, the agrarian background of Japanese society plays an important role in this regard.

As late as the early twentieth century, fully 80% of the Japanese population was engaged in subsistence-level rice farming; by 1945 more than half of all Japanese were still engaged in these laborious agricultural undertakings. Due to the shortage of land, Japanese rice farms operated quite differently from most of those outside Japan.

Rather than use up valuable space on each tract with housing for the farm family, as is the practice in the West, Japanese family rice farms were grouped together, with the families dividing a common farming area into "family" or "clan" rows. "For the Japanese peasant farmers," Lifson relates, "growing rice was a very precise life or death process."

As the individual rice farms abutted one another, usually without benefit of fences or formal boundaries, the only way one farmer could manage to keep his row straight was if his neighbor's row was also straight. Similarly, the use of flood-level watering that accompanies rice planting requires precise timing, with one farmer allowing the water to flow from his saturated field downhill to the parched and waiting field of his neighbor, then on to the next, and so on, always at just the right moment. With more than one hundred farms coordinating their activities in this manner, "mutual surveillance," says Lifson, "was absolutely necessary for survival."

Today, many Japanese do business much the same way their ancestors planted rice. They always have one eye on their own work and one eye on their neighbor's. This concept of mutual surveillance is endemic to Japanese organizational life, nowhere more so than in the area of decision-making.

Frequently, a Westerner will ask, when dealing with a new organization or sales prospect, "Who is the decision-maker in that shop?" In Japan, there is usually no decision-maker per se, only the decision-making process—a circular, holistic procedure that often mystifies and even offends outsiders. In some cases, however, this time-consuming process is quite appropriate and can yield better decisions, which are then implemented with higher levels of organizational gusto.

Linear versus Circular Decision-Making

Most non-Asians I've encountered tend to employ a linear approach to decision-making, grounded in the highly refined European and Greek systems of logic. Typically, this Western approach to problem-solving is characterized by top managers who move rationally toward a decision after they have reviewed and assessed the available information. The Japanese, however, tend to take the circular approach, going around and around within their group while working on honing consensus.

In the Japanese circular process, the same question is often asked more than once. Those who complain about this practice are not imagining things. However, what most non-Japanese usually fail to appreciate is that these repetitive questions typically come from different perspectives or contexts.

In fact, I've often heard Japanese colleagues criticize the Western decision-making process. Amused, they'll tell me, "You Westerners ask a question only once. You get an answer, you just assume that it is the full answer, and then you move down the decision-making process. You need to ask the same question many different times, in different contexts, in order to get a full appreciation of the problems and the full range of possible solutions."

In fact, an accurate answer to a given question might vary from time to time. In addition, the reason for asking a question, the motivation for a concern, can also shift over time, along with the responses. Thus, the circular decision-making process gathers data, at different time intervals, from as many points of view as possible. Up to a point, each time the decision-makers travel around the information-gathering circle the problem or opportunity comes into sharper focus, many strategies are developed and considered, and eventually, at some magic moment dictated more by the readiness of the group than by some external factor, like a deadline, a decision pops out.

This process can, of course, go on too long, as it frequently does in Japan. For example, each time American high-tech market leaders, like IBM, change technical standards there is almost always a lengthy delay in Japanese acceptance of those standards. Eventually, they make a decision, but it does take time. And in the meanwhile, American companies have a head start on their slower but more steady Japanese competition. A Japanese colleague illustrated this in a recent letter he wrote to me. "We have not succeeded in answering all of your problems," he wrote. "The answers we have found only serve to raise a whole new set of questions. In some ways, we feel we are as confused as ever, but we now believe we are confused on a much higher level and about more important things."

"We thought," an American colleague once told me in a similar vein, "that because they just kept asking the same questions month after month, that our Japanese partners were just being polite and didn't want to say 'no.' Boy, were we surprised when the answer came back 'yes.' We were certain it was a dead deal."

Oftentimes, Westerners figure their Japanese colleagues have had months with the relevant information and could have made a decision long ago. The Japanese, on the other hand, frequently take those months to refine, circulate, and evaluate the information, building the consensus that helps turn their management decisions into substantial company or group commitments.

In this area, I believe the decision-making performance of most non-Japanese managers can be greatly improved through the application, when appropriate, of the more inquisitive circular Japanese approach. Of course, some Western business leaders, CBS chairman Larry Tisch for one, are already renowned for their curiosity. However, Tisch's practice of asking endless streams of questions prior to making a major decision is so unheard of in the Western setting that it warranted substantial attention in a recent *Wall Street Journal* profile. In Japan, such practices are, for the most part, routine and not at all remarkable.

In fact, Western linear logic is often perceived as intrusive by the Japanese, who are apt to view it as an attempt to get inside their heads and do their thinking for them. If "A" leads inevitably to "B" the Japanese assume everyone is smart enough to figure that out for themselves. However, telling a Japanese associate that "A" leads to "B," without explaining in greater detail the reasons for that progression, often leaves the Japanese feeling they are being led down a path like children.

I've noticed that when my Japanese colleagues ask me for information they usually want data that are more detailed and more diverse than what most Westerners seek. My Japanese colleagues then dig deeply into this information but prefer to order the data themselves in a manner different from the Western way of thinking.

The difference relates mainly to the differing conceptions of logic. Although classic Greek logic, essential to most Westerners, is understood, it is not embraced by many Japanese. The Western logical, linear, one-step-at-a-time approach, many Japanese feel, represents an immature and impatient thought process. Instead, the Japanese subconscious, culturally based, circular logic technique is preferred.

It is not surprising, then, that business meetings in Japan are usually quite different from similar exercises in the West. In Japan, everybody is expected to already know the essential information, which has typically been previously shared well ahead of time as part of a regular communication process rooted in circular logic. It is almost as if the Japanese get together to confirm their reading of each other's minds, since they already know what is inside. Most of the people at one of these Japanese-style meetings will already know exactly what is to be discussed and the likely outcome. The purpose of the meeting is to create and strengthen a consensus.

Clearly, adherence to a rigid, "logical," time-driven agenda and the achievement of consensus represent quite opposite goals. The two do not mix well at all. Appreciating this aspect of reality has led me to the conclusion that artificial time pressures can have a great impact on managerial and company performance. As a result, I've learned to be more process-oriented and less deadline-driven. While deadlines can help focus energy and attention, the manager who has a clock for a master may find himself or herself marching punctually off in precisely the wrong direction.

As with the use of aggressive patience, I've also learned to separate problems into two groups when choosing between the Japanese circular or the Western linear decision-making process. Linear decision-making is, I've discovered, appropriate for tactical kinds of decisions, in which most of the data points are known, the environment is known, and the real need is to set priorities and assign tasks. Participating in a trade show, for example, is one type of problem that lends itself easily to linear decision-making. Either you go or you don't—and there is an absolute deadline involved. A linear-style yes or no does just fine.

Circular decision-making, on the other hand, is most appropriate in situations in which there are lots of variables and unknown information. In the circular process, we simply want to collect data, assemble facts, and see what emerges. Given this type of problem, developing a new marketing strategy, for instance, it is necessary to keep asking questions over and over until a clear direction is apparent.

I've often seen Japanese businesses hamstring themselves by applying the circular process to even the most simple linear type questions. I've also seen Western managers employ the hard-charging up-or-down yes-or-no linear process to questions that are too complex to be adequately addressed in that manner. The solution is to understand these two different decision-making styles and then apply the appropriate process in each situation. Simple questions can be answered simply; complicated questions demand the application of the more rigorous Japanese-style circular process.

Building the Consensus

The first step in the Japanese circular decision-making process is called *nemawashi,* which means, literally, "binding the roots before transplanting the tree." In business, this typically agrarian phrase refers to the one-on-one process by which consensus is developed in a Japanese organization prior to a formal decision. The agricultural metaphor of root-binding embodies laying the groundwork. Japanese society, with its long tradition of respecting accomplished horticulturalists, now routinely employs the nemawashi metaphor in a variety of nonagricultural, mainstream business settings.

In Japanese agriculture, when a tree (idea) is to be transplanted it is first dug up and some roots are cut. Strong rope is then wrapped around the roots and the tree is placed back in the ground for a year or longer to see if it survives. If it does, the tree can then be safely transplanted to another site. This metaphor has come to symbolize the Japanese need to meticulously prepare for any major new business initiative.

I first encountered nemawashi early in my experience with Japanese companies. At Toshiba, for example, the decision we made to introduce a fully IBM-compatible laptop computer in the U.S. market was heavily influenced by the nemawashi process.

Originally, Toshiba's products, like those of many other computer companies, were suffering in the marketplace because they were not fully IBM-compatible and could not run popular programs like Lotus 1-2-3 or Microsoft's Flight Simulator, two programs that seriously test PC clone IBM compatibility.

At an early juncture, it was obvious to those of us at Toshiba America that we had to be fully IBM-compatible. We had been living and breathing in the U.S. market and we knew what it required. But we had two other groups to contend with: the Japanese engineers in the Tokyo factory and the Tokyo marketing group. They were not so sure. They wondered if trading off some IBM compatibility for other features might better serve the customers, and by extension, the company. We knew better. But simply issuing a dictum to that effect was unthinkable. If our position was stated as a direct command, it would likely have been ignored or, even worse, could have generated considerable ill will. Telling someone what to do is a poor substitute for telling them why.

So, instead, we formed a study team, led by consultants

from McKinsey and Company, to go through the painstaking, and for us redundant, process of getting Toshiba's Japanese personnel talking to distributors, dealers, and end users, gathering data to help us decide what was needed. The study team was composed of all the constituencies at Toshiba, in America, in the Japanese factory, and in Toshiba's international sales and marketing division. Guess what the task force, composed of representatives from all these concerned divisions, concluded? We needed to be fully IBM-compatible.

Surprisingly, however, this exercise was very, very valuable. In fact, it turned out to be one of the most effective uses of an outside consultant I have encountered. Led collaboratively by McKinsey, but not dictated or directed by them, our study team was able to form and then strongly endorse its own conclusions. McKinsey's consultants did not "solve" our problem; they helped us solve our problem by facilitating a consensus across country borders and company divisions.

The purpose of the task force was, of course, to get the others to buy into the decision, which did seem to me at the time to be a royal waste of time. But I learned that in the end, it wasn't. When the other groups bought in, they bought in with a vengeance, and their commitment more than made up for the slow decision-making. When we finally settled on the idea of being "Blue" (IBM's color) all the players felt they owned the idea. We were then all equally determined to be a "brighter Blue."

In Japan, this nemawashi process is usually coupled with the formalized Japanese *ringi* system, whereby all of those affected by a change affix their personal seal, literally, to planning documents that are circulated prior to any major business decision. In actual nemawashi practice, though, an informal approval of all key individuals is sought before any plan is formally proposed. Therefore, rejection of a proposal in the ringi phase is relatively rare.

In most companies, the ringi form is used merely to formalize and acknowledge the development of consensus. It is a bottom-up document; approval is first sought from the bottom of the company ladder and then moves up the organizational chart. The top manager is usually the last, not the first, to agree to any major business decision. Memos and ideas of this sort are not handed down from on-high. They bubble up.

This process certainly takes time, but the goal is to get everyone to buy into a decision before it is implemented, in part, so that if there is a failure, it is a group failure. Given this inclusive style, it is much easier to actually make and implement the most aggressive decisions. The time lost on this process can turn out to be time very well spent.

In the nemawashi practice, the person responsible for an area of the business draws up a plan and then, one-on-one, circulates it to all of those likely to be affected: colleagues, people in related departments, and superiors. If someone does not approve, the idea is modified or withdrawn. These nemawashi sessions are almost always conducted in private because the Japanese are very conscious of offending or embarrassing one another. Free from the worry of shaming a colleague by challenging ideas in public or pointing out an overlooked item, these private nemawashi sessions serve instead to sharpen the idea and build a constituency for its implementation. Acting on the criticism leveled in a private, one-on-one session might save an idea that would otherwise have been tabled by the same objection brought up at a later date.

In the United States we like to say it is important "to get all our ducks in line." For most Japanese managers, that is not enough. Instead, they try to get all their ducks lined up and marching in the same direction for the same reasons. It is not that they have smarter ducks. Instead, they have a different system aimed at building consensus at every turn.

Most non-Japanese managers I've encountered can certainly stand to increase consensus-building in their organizations. In Japan, this is usually done reflexively, as part of their daily interpersonal interactions. Those outside Japan need to work harder to achieve this goal. Company newsletters, for example, are an often underused forum in which company decisions and activities can be presented and discussed more thoroughly. Regular, informal roundtable discussions with employees or a weekly management open-door forum are also good ways to get people started on a path toward consensus. However, it is important not to go too far down this path. Trying to build absolute consensus, as Japanese managers often do, can reach a point of diminishing return. Instead, work toward consensus with the goal of reaching a state of collaboration.

Moving from Consensus to Collaboration

I've learned that reaching 100% consensus when managing a company, as the Japanese strive to do, is often not the most effective approach. Most non-Japanese are simply unwilling, or unable, to devote the time required for the extensive one-on-one nemawashi sessions that are needed to get everyone to agree to a decision. Nonetheless, when I'm reviewing a decision made by one of my subordinates, I do usually insist on their at least talking to all the people and constituencies involved with the decision. Doing so, of course, helps avoid creating a group of alienated workers or colleagues.

In fact, I am often amazed when I ask questions of my managers, such as, "Well, did you talk to the sales manager?" and the answer comes back, "No, he was out of town," or, I ask, "Did you talk to the MIS director?" "No, I didn't have time." So many decisions get made in these kinds of information vacuums it is small wonder results often fail to meet expectations. In my experience, Westerners seem to have a real problem collaborating with colleagues systematically, with all of those who will be affected by a decision. This is especially true if it is feared that some other parties might have a different opinion on the subject at hand.

By insisting that a decision-maker collaborate in an open-minded fashion with all constituents prior to a decision it is possible to powerfully reinforce whatever decision is eventually made. However, by giving the decision-maker the power to make the decision when the time is right, even without consensus, a collaborative process, in between authoritarian dictation and paralytic total consensus can emerge.

Experience tells me that this collaborative decision-making technique, somewhere in between the Western autocratic approach and the Japanese consensus style, works best. While developing the consensus approach requires 100% effort to achieve 100% buy-in, a collaborative approach can require only about 20% effort and still achieve 80% buy in. Put another way, for roughly one-fifth of the effort it takes to get everyone to agree, you can usually get around 80% agreement. Even those who are unconvinced will appreciate and respond to the effort made to include them in the final decision.

Certainly, talking with and involving all of the people involved in the decision-making process is one of the best ways to avoid the alienation of labor that Karl Marx fretted so much about. People want to be heard, not dictated to. If they own the decision, if it is as much theirs as yours, it becomes impossible to excuse later performance deficits with the standard "it wasn't my idea" excuse. It *was* their idea.

It is important to note that a commitment to this inclusive decision-making style is required across the board, not just for major, earth-shaking decisions. For example, when the time came for us to change our business card logo and design I asked our marketing communications group to come up with several alternatives. We then presented those designs at our executive staff meeting. The ten participants took just five minutes to note their top two choices. I then took that information into consideration and, along with the marketing team, made a decision that was actually somewhat contradictory to the vote we had taken, but still well within the general approval range, sort of settling on what was at least most people's second choice. In the end, the decision was respected, even popular, in part because it considered the input of everyone who would be affected. Everyone involved knew that if they'd had a strong objection, it would have been heard.

Practicing this collaborative decision-making style for even the most routine matters, like selecting a business card design, helps debug an organization of its autocratic impulses. In addition, I also use this approach when any new employee joins our organization. Prior to hire, I insist the prospective employee be interviewed by all the colleagues, supervisors, and constituencies involved. Those people then have more ownership of that hiring decision than would be the case if the new person just shows up for work one morning.

Ideally, if you can turn managerial decisions into group decisions, you can get group ownership and group performance. The best leaders, in any country, are those who get everyone to do what they want, and to think they are doing so because it was their idea.

Delegate Authority, Not Responsibility

The way responsibility is shouldered in an organization can have a large influence on the effectiveness of the decision-making process. Many Japanese point to retired Chrysler executive Lee Iaccoca as an amusing example of Western managerial shortcomings in this regard. When, for example, some Chrysler employees were caught turning back the odometer on used models that were sold as new,

Iaccoca promptly announced that he didn't know anything about the practice and wasn't involved. He quickly fired those he judged to have been responsible and, having done so, asked the public to once again put their trust in Chrysler's products. Indeed, Iaccoca's actions seem typical for many CEOs and top managers facing a crisis, a misdeed, or a drastic drop in sales: Pinpoint blame, fire the guy, and then pretend it never happened.

Most Japanese executives, facing a similar ordeal, would likely have resigned or, at the very least, taken personal responsibility and apologized. After all, the executive hired and managed the people who made that mistake. Who knows, then, what mistakes others hired by the same person are making in different but equally vital areas?

In fact, and while it is a practice much too extreme to be emulated, certainly not more than once, dozens of Japanese executives commit suicide each year in their apologetic assumption of responsibility for culturally shameful business setbacks. While this practice is, thankfully, waning, the recent contraction in the Japanese economy has resulted in scores of top-level resignations from Japanese banking, real estate, and securities firms. When the American stock market crashed in October 1987, few Wall Street top executives felt the impact although many lower-level workers lost jobs. In Japan, many of these top firms now have completely new management.

Even when a train crashes in Japan, the head of the railroad company will usually quit, his career forever tarnished by his failure to pick better employees. Similarly, in a recent well-publicized incident, a senior Japanese news writer at Kyodo News Service admitted to plagiarizing a series of articles on health matters. Not only was he quickly fired, but his bosses took it on the chin; the managing editor resigned his post, four other senior editors lost titles or took pay cuts, and even the top dog, the president of the news agency, got involved, announcing that he personally was taking a temporary pay cut to show contrition for the episode.

In contrast, when GM announced that business setbacks necessitated the closing of 21 plants and the layoff of 74,000 workers, not one senior GM executive cut his high salary. Although some bonuses were reduced, the compensation for GM's failing top executives still exceeds, by far, the salaries paid to executives at the more successful Japanese auto companies.

As I've often been told by my Japanese colleagues, "In the United States, decision-making is centralized and responsibility is diffused. In Japan, decision-making is diffused and responsibility is centralized." If something goes wrong in Japan, the pain starts, symbolically, at the top and works its way down the ranks, not the other way. This reality puts additional although subtle pressure on employees not to let their bosses down; they might embarrass their own supervisor and, by so doing, shame themselves.

In a typical Japanese organization there is never any doubt about who bears ultimate responsibility. Indeed, in many Japanese companies, the top position is largely a ceremonial role, presided over by a prestigious functionary who does little save greet visitors, serve as a figurehead, and, when necessary, assume total responsibility. At the same time, considerable authority is vested in individual employees.

While consensus decision-making is the norm in most Japanese companies, once a decision is made, employees are usually given considerable latitude about how they implement that decision. Mindful of their obligation to superiors, empowered employees, even in what may appear to be insignificant positions, are then able to impress others by reaching agreed upon goals in novel, sometimes quite creative ways.

In fact, one of the most common complaints Westerners

make about top Japanese bosses is that they often have very little to say in group meetings. Instead, most of the talking is done by underlings, each concentrating on their area of responsibility. Often, the Japanese boss, if she or he is there, will not say a word in between "It's nice to meet you" and "goodbye." Sometimes, the Japanese boss may even appear to be dozing in the middle of a meeting! Although rare, given the Japanese practice of occasionally closing their eyes tightly when concentrating, such an event is not unprecedented.

Rather than signify disinterest, however, such behavior usually indicates the Japanese executive's trust in the ability of his or her subordinates. This dichotomy, in which a Japanese manager delegates authority but not responsibility, provides employees with a kind of safety net above which they can securely perform the business equivalent of aerobatic stunts. Relieved of the worry that they and they alone will be held responsible for a mishap or mistake, it becomes easier to experiment with new approaches.

Similarly, knowing that they will be held directly responsible for the behavior of all of those under their charge, typical Japanese managers have no stomach for letting employees fail. The best managers are those who stay involved with their employees at all times, monitoring, mentoring, providing feedback, and vesting authority. Doing so without relinquishing responsibility is the best way to model the appropriate behavior.

Nonadversarial Negotiations

Formal negotiations are the quintessential form of decision-making. As anyone with Japanese/Western cross-cultural experience can attest, negotiations usually proceed quite differently in Japan. I've personally participated in hundreds of negotiating sessions with my Japanese colleagues and have learned at least one important thing. They do not begin when they start and they are not over when they are finished. In contrast to most negotiations in the West, negotiations in Japan are not discrete events. Instead, they are a natural extension of all relationship-building, all consensus decision-making, all strategic uses of silence to communicate, and all patient, diligent preparation.

Perhaps the biggest difference between an average Western and an average Japanese negotiating session can be found in the goal. While it is not always the case, Western negotiators usually hope to win, which means the other side, more or less, must lose. This adversarial posture, combined with the very non-Japanese Western practice of separating negotiations from most other more routine business interactions, can create a contentious atmosphere.

Most of my negotiations with Japanese colleagues have been quite different. The goal is almost always explicitly understood: Both sides must win. Long discussions and huge amounts of information-sharing take place, sometimes interminably. Japanese negotiators will often stay at the table, or at the bar or restaurant, exploring every little detail of a deal, going over it again and again while looking for ways to fashion a more mutually beneficial outcome.

University of California at Irvine professor John Graham, who studies negotiating styles across cultures, confirmed these observations in one of his most recent experiments. He set up a negotiating game in which two groups of negotiators, one American and one Japanese, were given an identical task: Each group was divided into two subgroups, buyers and sellers, and were then given a price/profit schedule for a mock inventory of appliances they were to sell or buy within their group. The result: The American negotiators played their cards very close to their vests, with the sellers and buyers not telling each other, in any detail, which prices would result in acceptable levels of profit and why. They negotiated as if it were a numerical parlor game, putting out numbers without much explanation and, eventually, agreeing to transactions that did not maximize the potential profits available to both parties in this complicated exercise.

The Japanese negotiating team approached the problem quite differently. They shared nearly all of the information they had about their mock inventories and explored in detail which prices for which items would result in greater profits for both buyers and sellers. Even though they started out with identical mock inventories, when the Japanese team was finished they had arrived at a set of transactions that resulted in more profits for both buyers and sellers. The difference—a rather large one in this exercise—provides evidence that nonadversarial negotiations are clearly preferable to win-lose negotiations.

Additionally, if both sides win it is more likely they can, and will, do business together again. And of course, that should be the goal, not a one-time win-lose but rather the creation of an extended series of win-wins.

Negotiating in this manner means not only stating your position, but explaining and defending, in great detail, the reasons for that position. Finding mutually agreeable solutions becomes much easier once the reasons for a given position are on the table alongside the position or demand. In recent years, some very good books, *Getting to Yes* among them, have tried to move the Western business negotiating style closer to this win-win model.

Unfortunately, however, many negotiators are still stuck in the old adversarial mode, particularly in the West. Sometimes, the exploration of win-win solutions is even used as a mere ploy aimed at tricking an adversary into accepting an inferior proposition. In actual practice, however, nonadversarial negotiations work only if there is an absolutely sincere desire to make sure that your adversary walks away from the negotiations as a genuine winner, not just thinking they have won.

This is, of course, not to say that Japanese negotiators do not look for and exploit weaknesses during negotiations. They certainly do. Graham, in another of his studies, confirmed this by asking groups of Japanese and American managers what attributes they feel are important in their negotiators. While there is room to argue whether these answers represent tatamae or honne positions, the contrast is interesting.

Managers' Rating of Preferred Attributes of Negotiators

American/Western	*Japanese*
1. Preparation and planning	Dedication to task
2. Thinking under pressure	Integrity
3. Judgment and intelligence	Perceive and exploit power
4. Verbal expression	Win respect and confidence
5. Product knowledge	Verbal expression
6. Perceive and exploit power	Open-minded
7. Integrity	Listening skill

For the Japanese managers who responded to Graham's study, perceiving and exploiting power was clearly a key component of negotiating. However, it is worth noting that, for the Japanese, this adversarial posture follows integrity and dedication in order of importance. For the Americans, by their own admission, integrity was far less important, ranking last, while thinking under pressure and being fast on their feet were considered more vital, presumably to gain some advantage in what is assumed to be an adversarial process.

Of course, studies like those done by Graham can only skim the surface when it comes to measuring the differences in negotiations in the West and in Japan. His basic conclusions, however, that Japanese negotiators share more information and work harder and longer to find mutually beneficial solutions, does match much personal experience.

Strangely enough, I've found a win-win negotiating style to be useful in some quite unexpected ways. For example, I recently had to terminate a very senior employee. I approached this unpleasant task by presenting the employee with the idea that we needed to find a way to continue our longstanding business relationship. To do so, we needed to find out the real needs of each party. The real needs of the company were to move that employee out, and quickly, but to do it in a gracious manner that was perceived as fair by the rest of the company.

The real need of the employee was an acceptable one-time severance package and the preservation of his reputation. We settled on a good package: severance pay combined with the announcement of an ongoing consulting agreement. I also agreed to introduce the employee to other parts of the parent organization and provided related character references. The key was to create the understanding that I wanted to preserve an important relationship. What could easily have become a contentious wrongful termination suit turned out, instead, to have a far happier ending for both parties.

Ideally, a climate conducive to constructive, collaborative negotiations should be created before any formal negotiations begin. In most instances, if you wait until the start of formal negotiations to commence relationship-building, if you do not share information freely, and if you insist on defeating your adversary, you will probably wind up the bigger loser in the fullness of time.

Alchemist's Tool Kit #7
Making a Decision Checklist

AMERICAN/WESTERN

Linear decision-making—
spot or conclude logic

Authoritative/participative
decision-making

Pacesetting management
style

Top-down decision-making
process

Delegates authority and
responsibility

Negotiating attributes:
Preparation and planning
Thinking under pressure
Judgment and intelligence
Verbal expression
Product knowledge
Perceive and exploit
power
Integrity

Highly value rational skills
in negotiating

JAPANESE

Circular decision-making—
collective or assembly
logic

Participative/consensus
decision-making

Coaching management style

Bottom-up decision-making
process

Delegates authority, not
responsibility

Negotiating attributes:
Dedication to task
Integrity
Perceive and exploit
power
Win respect and
confidence
Verbal expression
Open-minded
Listening skills

Highly value process skills
in negotiating

MANAGEMENT TIPS

- Use aggressive patience to move the decision-making process along. Be patient enough to insure that you explore all the alternatives from all different contexts.

- The concept of aggressive patience requires an individual to "own the problem." Clearly define who has ownership in bringing the situation to closure over an extended period of time.

- Understand the circular decision-making process; explore alternatives over and over, ask questions, get data even if you do not know where they will lead. Remember what drives demand for Japanese wooden tubs.

- Do not be forced into making hasty decisions by a linear decision-making process that goes from A to B, and only asks the same question once. Make decisions when you have the best results, not just when the calendar dictates.

- Linear decision-making is usually best for tactical issues. Circular decision-making is most appropriate for strategic decisions; use both of them whenever appropriate.

- Get others to "own" your ideas. Use nemawashi techniques to win support and transplant your ideas to your colleagues.

- Get all your ducks marching in the same direction for the same reasons. Do not expect to achieve total consensus; practice collaborative management where you can get 80% of your colleague's ownership with 20% of effort and time.

- Delegate authority, never responsibility.

- Strive for a win-win negotiating result in the context of a long-term relationship, in which each party understands the other's real needs, rather than a short-term win-lose result.

- Be a nonadversarial negotiator. Share information and understand the difference between rational techniques and process techniques in negotiating. Create a good balance between the two.

8

PUTTING THE PERFORMANCE HORSE BEFORE THE FISCAL CART:

Making the Start-Up Mode Permanent

American entrepreneurs are widely admired in Japan. Indeed, many of the United States' most famous entrepreneurs have relied on Japanese capital and technical support to build their companies. Apple Computer co-founder Steve Jobs, for example, was so respected in Japan that the venerable Canon corporation quickly coughed up $100 million to buy a minority position in his ill-fated NeXT Computer company. The sizable investment was made well before NeXT even had a product ready for sale.

According to JETRO, Japan's External Trade and Research Organization, there are more than 1,500 similar joint ventures between American and Japanese companies in an average year. Although some of these arrangements are between big companies, many of them take place between smaller American entrepreneurial start-ups and large Japanese conglomerates. In general, Japanese executives tell me they have come to expect a high level of vibrancy within the U.S. entrepreneurial ranks. I suspect this is probably because the management style in a typical start-up business looks familiar to my colleagues in Japan; it is largely similar to the way they try to do business all the time. In the future, this entrepreneurial model will become even more important.

Most managers in established firms learned long ago that they must compete not only with each other but also with the new kids on the block, the start-up enterprises that are grabbing market share not with brute force but with cunning and smart hands-on management. Short cycle time in decision-making and product development generally characterizes these entrepreneurial companies. The affinity between American start-ups and huge Japanese conglomerates might seem odd at first. But it is not a mismatch. Instead, the similarities between the two are quite real. Understanding these similarities is important because they prove that all managers, whether in large or midsize companies, can learn to run their operations in an entrepreneurial mode. In the future, doing so is more than wise; it is imperative.

One of the most important similarities between U.S. start-ups and large Japanese businesses concerns the expressed goals of top management. Most successful entrepreneurs start their businesses with a very specific focus. The best of them usually set precise targets in terms of customers and markets. This same specificity of focus also exemplifies most of the large Japanese companies I've encountered.

Like entrepreneurs, Japanese managers generally use the most aggressive of terms when referring to their business objectives: They "encircle" the competition with better products; they take "countermeasures" to reduce negative variances to budget; they try to "capture" a given market. The mission statements or company slogans of these businesses usually reflect this orientation. They, too, are usually very precise, even militaristic on occasion. For example, the team that developed the Toyota Supra was known internally as the "Porsche Killers." Similarly, the Nissan product development team had a clear mission, embodied in its combination moniker/mission statement: "Beat Benz." The Komatsu tractor company made no bones about its mission: "Encircle Caterpillar" read the sign on the lunchroom wall.

In contrast, in the West, and particularly in the United States, many of the slogans or mission statements, especially those used by large companies, are often so vague and mealy-mouthed they could be exchanged among firms without anyone ever noticing. "To serve the public" or "to be the best in the field" are phrases that make frequent appearances in Western corporate slogans.

While there are exceptions, such as Ford's clearly stated goal (implemented with a more than $1,000 price reduction) of matching its Taurus model against arch competitor Nissan, for the most part Western corporate mission statements usually convey very little of what is, or at least what should be, on the agenda of the company's top leaders. Instead, they are usually rife with vague metaphors drawn from the sports world, often with little or no relevance or reference to the company's actual real-world competitors or true goals. It often seems that Western sales managers are the only group who are accustomed to making regular references to their competition.

A more specific focus enumerated by top management and embraced by all employees characterizes both large Japanese firms as well as U.S. entrepreneurial companies. These companies give their workers and investors a clear message: Beat the competition. Despite the combative vocabulary, though, several Japanese managers have told me they know business is not war. It is more like a marathon race, they say, in which attention to kaizen constantly pushes the finishing line out of reach.

Unfortunately, the American financial culture sometimes pushes companies out of the entrepreneurial mode too quickly. For example, the A. T. Kearney company recently surveyed managers in both Japan and the United States, asking what stockholders wanted most from their companies. By a large margin, American managers said their stockholders were most interested in increased stock value, company growth, and company stability, in that order. Japanese managers, in contrast, replied that their stockholders were interested in company growth first, company stability second, and increased stock value last.

This difference is quite important. Indeed, I have no idea how the American business leaders surveyed intend to increase their stock value, over the long term, without first concentrating on insuring the growth and stability of their companies. This survey, however, confirms the darkest fears derived from my personal observations: too many managers have put the fiscal cart before the performance horse. It is a strategy doomed to fail.

Entrepreneurs, on the other hand, know they must sacrifice to build their companies. This recognition helps explain why Japanese executives are often more comfortable working with foreign start-ups, no matter how shaky they might be, rather than with larger, finance-driven firms. Start-ups usually have everything at risk and act accordingly. This attitude, unlike the complacency often found in larger companies, is comfortingly familiar to most Japanese executives.

Another survey done by the same organization was also revealing. Top Japanese business leaders are on average twice as concerned with building market share than are Americans, five times more focused on new product development, and only minimally concerned with return on investment or shareholder value. Over the long term, there is no debate about which of these perspectives is the better approach.

As these studies confirm, most Japanese managers tend

to operate under the assumption that increased stock value is the result of market development and company growth. This will occur, of course, only if a company is stable. If these factors are present, the Japanese manager reasons that stock prices will eventually take care of themselves. If these factors are not present, no amount of balance sheet smoke and mirrors will ever make up the difference.

Japan's 1992 stock market slide demonstrates how closely tied the Japanese financial markets are to issues of day-to-day company performance. Unlike in the West, when a Japanese company suffers a slowdown in sales, which most major Japanese companies have endured during the recent global recession, the company's stock almost always declines. This also happens in the United States, of course. However, almost as often, and up to a certain point, stock prices of American companies rise on bad news. "Sell on good news and buy on bad news," is, of course, a well-worn piece of American stockbroker advice. The reasoning usually goes something like this: The company has taken its hit, bit the bullet, downsized appropriately, and is now poised for a good quarter. As Japan's 1992 stock market collapse demonstrated, these familiar assurances carry little weight in Tokyo. Japan's investment community is impressed by growing markets and margins, not by optimistic assurances about countermeasures like downsizing or one-time writeoffs.

The important question is how we can encourage managers and employees, wherever they are located, to stay focused on the long-term goals of their companies, such as growth and stability, despite short-term pressures. Even in Japan, these short-term considerations are now threatening to undermine future growth and prosperity.

Meeting this challenge requires that managers act as if they are entrepreneurs. They must define the specific missions of their companies, set the right examples, develop strategic relationships with employees and business partners, and provide customers with the very best in customer service and support. Most Japanese companies already pay very close attention to these areas, as do most successful entrepreneurs. By focusing on these tasks, managers can forward their company's long-term objectives notwithstanding the short-term pressures they must always confront.

It Starts at the Top

I am frequently amazed by the lack of understanding many managers evidence regarding the symbolism of their daily activities. Unlike entrepreneurs, who generally set the right example in this respect out of sheer necessity, many managers I've known seem to think their rank entitles them to work less diligently than their subordinates. Of course, the exact opposite is true. It is important for managers to realize that their tenure depends largely on recognizing the responsibility they have to model the appropriate behavior on the job.

For starters, I always encourage my managers to get to work before their subordinates arrive and to be there to wish their charges goodnight as they leave. Typically, this means a 8:00 A.M. to 6:30 P.M. work day. In addition, I encourage them to show discipline in their lunch breaks and try to stick to the same lunch hours as their employees.

A common defensive retort is, "I'm doing my job, getting it done, so I don't need to work those hours," or "It's a privilege of my position that I can go home or leave the office early on a regular basis." The question I come back with is, "Well, what is your job? What exactly *is* the job of a manager?"

Organizational development experts I've consulted with tell me workplace studies reveal that roughly 85% of a manager's behavior is transferred directly to subordinates, affecting their actions, attitudes, and productivity. It does not matter what managers say; it is what they *do* that really counts.

As a rule, Japanese managers put in more hours than their American counterparts. A recent study of managerial work loads in Japan and the United States, for example, concluded that Japanese managers, on average, put in the equivalent of 52 full 40-hour work weeks per year, considerably more time on the job than the average American manager. While Juliet Schor's bestselling book, *The Overworked American,* revealed that employed Americans are, in general, working more hours than at any time since the Great Depression, American managers do not put in the hours most Japanese managers devote to their labors. Only American entrepreneurs can match the average Japanese manager in their level of dedication.

Of course, statistical comparisons across decades and countries are always difficult. How do you make a meaningful statistical comparison between a manual typist and a word processor operator, for example? And how do you include nonoffice, honne-style interactions with colleagues in such calculations?

Statistics aside, it is clear that most Western managers could certainly set a better example for their subordinates. In Japan, setting this example is a routine and expected part of a manager's job, and its absence is a rare occurrence. Outside Japan, however, I've frequently had problems with managers who seem unaware of or unconcerned about the damage their personal work habits can do to company morale.

In the West, a leader is usually someone with a strong ego, often with a kind of charisma that allows the person to take charge, make decisions, and assume responsibility without being bothered by more mundane things, like consulting with subordinates. This kind of charismatic leader would flounder in most Japanese companies, destroying essential harmony and team spirit. Most Japanese managers seem to know instinctively that their job is to inspire, to lead, and to set an example.

Interestingly, a recent Korn Ferry study of leadership traits across national boundaries revealed that integrity and intelligence were expected attributes of leaders both in Japan and the United States. However, the Japanese were the only group who also listed physical fitness as being a key requirement in their leaders. This is probably because physical fitness is a measure of personal discipline. And personal discipline, knowing what to do and when to do it and having the strength it takes to resist impulsive moves, is an indication that an individual has the inner strength required to be a good leader in the Japanese context.

The Western penchant for charismatic leaders stands in contrast to the Japanese requirement that leaders possess considerable patience and be able to achieve group consensus and harmony by listening carefully to others. Leadership, Japanese-style, requires self-control, discipline, and patience.

The consequences of the example established by top management are important even if they are frequently incalculable: How much company productivity and team spirit are squandered when employees feel they are being led by managers who lack commitment to their work? What happens, for example, when employees arrive for work on time only to find the best spots in the parking lot reserved for executives who have not yet showed up. What a great way to start a day! Really makes you want to pitch in and grab that ringing phone before taking a break, right? Wrong.

Little things set the tone and establish the culture within a company. Some successful American companies which, interestingly, are also thriving in Japan, like Lisle, Illinois' Molex Corporation, for example, have become well known for the way their top management inspires employees to higher levels of dedication. At Molex, the top officers, most of them members of the tightknit Krehbiel family, are noted for getting to work even before the janitors arrive. There are no reserved spots in the Molex parking lot despite the company's location in the heart of the often frigid American Midwest. Nevertheless, on any given day, the best parking spots are usually occupied by the company's top managers, who compete with each other for the best spots in the company lot by getting to work early.

Unfortunately, such practices are so noteworthy in American companies that when they do occur they generate considerable attention, admiration, and in the case of Molex, magazine articles. In most Japanese companies, this leadership by example is the rule, not the exception. Of course, in some cases, where both parents work, for example, family needs may compel a manager to leave work early from time to time. However, I make certain my managers understand that the symbolism and behavior example they set are the most important parts of their job. If, for family reasons, they must leave early now and then, I expect them to make up for those absences in a very visible way. In my experience, far too many Western managers regard their rank as a license to do things less, not more, assiduously than do the "worker bees."

Seiko Instruments, USA, has a policy of always using off-airport parking whenever an employee travels. Over a year, this policy can save a considerable amount of money, as parking lots just a few minutes from an airport generally are half as expensive. On more than one occasion, their senior American employees violated this policy, typically offering the excuse that they were in a hurry or had already saved the company money by getting a discounted airplane ticket. The very highest-ranking Japanese managers, in contrast, rigorously follow this policy, regardless of their rank or status.

When I drove to the airport with one of Seiko Instruments, USA's, top Japanese officials there is never any question; we head for the cheap parking lot. That is the company policy, across the board, and top Japanese management would simply never dream of violating the policy and adding an unnecessary expense account expenditure. I often tell my subordinates that managers seem to judge themselves by their intentions ("it's okay to violate the parking policy because I saved the company money in other ways") while they judge others by their actions ("they better follow the policy"). Actions matter most. Senior managers should remember that their employees judge them by their actions, too.

Likewise, in many companies rank determines which managers fly coach, which fly first-class, and which fly by charter or private company jet. It is pretty hard to convince employees of the need for financial efficiencies when a management flight that could have cost $500 instead runs $1,000 or $1,500. The predictable subconscious response of employees is to find their own ways to get even by wasting even greater sums of company money whenever possible. When Seiko Instruments, USA, hit some turbulent financial waters a few years ago we decided that everyone, myself included, would fly coach, even on international flights. In reality, the money didn't matter all that much. But the symbolism did. The responsibility for establishing a culture of dedication begins at the top. Employees pay more attention to what managers do than what they say. You should, too.

Flat Organizations

Another key similarity between America's entrepreneurial start-ups and many Japanese companies is what has been called the flat management approach. In most large American companies, conventional wisdom has it that no more than seven to nine people can be effectively supervised by any one manager. This leads, inevitably, to pyramid-style organizational charts. Most entrepreneurs, however, have no use for these pyramids. They are more comfortable talking with whomever needs to be talked with and doing whatever needs to be done at any given moment.

Similarly, in most thriving Japanese businesses the number of direct reports is usually closer to 15 or 20, sometimes even more. Even so, these managers are usually able to stay on top of all the functional areas under their supervision.

For example, one of the best bosses I ever had was Mr. K. Ishiguro, who served as president of Toshiba America and, as such, was responsible for five Toshiba divisions. As the person responsible for all these separate business lines, Mr. Ishiguro constantly wanted to know everything that was going on in each division. So he made a point of asking just that, not only of senior managers like myself, but of nearly everyone. He was always determined to get whatever information he needed directly from the line source. Mr. Ishiguro had no use whatsoever for middle managers whose main job function was to tell him what their subordinates were thinking. Mr. Ishiguro felt more comfortable finding out those things for himself.

The most important lesson Mr. Ishiguro taught me is that top management sets the proper example by keeping well informed, through many different channels, about what is going on in their organizations. In Japan, managers are rarely brought in from the outside to solve a particular problem or crisis. Instead, the Japanese manager has usually been rotated in after holding a variety of jobs in the company. By rotating through many key jobs, usually switching positions every three years or so, the Japanese manager gains an appreciation for and experience with the various tasks that confront his or her organization. This is not to suggest that top management then stops delegating and gets involved in every little detail. Instead, the detailed knowledge of what is going on allows the manager to act more decisively when problems do arise.

In contrast, the American managerial pattern often appears bloated. McKinsey and Company's managing director for Japan, Kenichi Ohmae, for example, had this to say about General Motors in a recent *Wall Street Journal* article: "The big three auto makers are unquestionably suffering because of the recession. But even in the most buoyant economy, GM is still a very inefficient maker of cars. In 1991, the company employed more than 400,000 people in the U.S. to make roughly 4.2 million cars. In the same year, Toyota employed only 97,000 people to produce more than 4.2 million cars and trucks."

According to Ohmae, many of the unneeded workers can be found in the middle management ranks. In fact, studies have revealed that American auto companies have, on average, more than twice as many levels of management than do their Japanese competitors. Clearly, there is really very little need for managers whose primary task is brokering information within a company.

Flat management is especially effective in sales organizations. If, for example, top management stays informed regarding how individual sales team members are performing, by asking them directly, then the sales manager can concentrate on selling product to major customers rather than spending valuable time preparing sales reports and the like.

At Seiko Instruments, USA, we cut about 15 middle management positions, out of approximately 350 employees, and found that doing so increased the efficiency of the organization. We concentrated on supporting those workers who actually get the job done by eliminating managerial positions that served solely to convey information from one level to another within the organization. In this respect, less really is more.

Members of the sales team admit that before the streamlining, information on their problems and their assessment of sales forecasts and market size were often lost in the middle management communications shuffle. There is now much better communication between top management and the sales force and more accurate "bottoms up" sales forecasting.

In Japan, the ka or section is a key building block of the flat organization. The kacho or section head usually has at least 15 people working for him or her, often more. Typically, a manager receives the kacho assignment after 10 or 15 years with the company. The kacho knows the jobs of each subordinate since, in most cases, he or she held each of those jobs before getting a promotion. Likewise, due to the open offices in most Japanese companies, the subordinates are exposed to the kacho on a daily basis and have an appreciation of the kacho's responsibilities. Broad two-way communication is encouraged.

The high number of people reporting directly to the kacho also helps empower the entire workforce. Since it really is impossible for a supervisor to micromanage 20 or more people, more delegation of authority (but never responsibility) usually takes place. In this kind of environment, the temptation of a manager to micromanage a small cadre of workers is supplanted by macromanagement—setting goals, offering inspiration, and keeping the channels of communication open. This gives employees more freedom than they might otherwise enjoy while maintaining their accountability to the company.

Customer Service

It is in their mutual dedication to customer service that entrepreneurs and the best Japanese managers have the most in common. Entrepreneurs know the customer is everything. In a start-up, there is no business without satisfied customers. There is simply no room for error.

Most of the Japanese managers I've worked with also regard customer service as the lifeblood of their businesses. No stone is left unturned when it comes to helping customers. Japanese managers regularly use customer service as a marketing tool, in part, because keeping existing customers happy is one of the best ways to find new customers. Japanese managers will frequently go to extraordinary lengths to demonstrate their dedication to customers, both existing and potential.

For example, not long ago I was invited to speak at a seminar co-sponsored by the Japan America Society and the Japan Development Bank. Shortly after agreeing to the invitation, I got a call from the managing director of the bank. He requested an appointment. A few days later, he and his associate arrived at my office after a three-hour roundtrip drive from their headquarters. The purpose: They wanted to thank me, in advance, for agreeing to speak at their conference.

Over the years, I have taken part in more than 100 panels and speaking engagements and this was the first time somebody drove out to personally thank me for my effort. It seemed remarkable to me. For the bank officials, though, it was just another day at the office, doing one of the things the Japanese do best: customer service. Although I was not a customer, building a personal relationship with me and others like me is part of the bank's official marketing strategy.

At Seiko Instruments, USA, I made visiting customers a requirement of all senior managers. In order to earn their bonuses, senior managers are required to visit a predetermined number of customers each month. Personally, I visit at least 4 customers per month. Sometimes these visits help close a big sale or solve an individual problem. In every single instance, however, I've learned something important from these visits, information ranging from how our products are being used to how well our service staff is doing their job.

When visiting customers, I always try and spend some time with them in their own private offices. This is a very good way to get to know these customers better; you notice the pictures on their desk and any signs of personal hobbies or interests. You get a much better sense of these customers as people and become more attuned to their individual needs and requirements. Often, when I ask my senior managers to respond personally to a customer complaint they'll try and bump the task down to more junior employees. I discourage this whenever possible. It seems pretty simple, but if, as a manager, you want to know how good a job of customer service your people are doing, go ask the customer yourself.

Of course, some Western companies have already discovered that excellent customer service is the surest path to success. The Men's Wearhouse, for example, a fast-growing discount clothing chain in the United States, calls every single customer who buys more than a tie within a week of purchase to ask them if they were treated properly. Unfortunately, despite all the attention it has received, this kind of effort is still exceedingly rare outside Japan.

Seiko Instruments, USA, also routinely called customers, thanks them for their business, and asked their opinions about products and services. We also took full advantage of the chance to gather information from any calls that came to us. For instance, like most high-tech companies, Seiko gets a few thousand calls to the technical support center each month. In addition to helping solve whatever technical support problem motivated the call, we also asked callers where they purchased Seiko Instruments' product, if they were/are satisfied with services, and if they have any ideas regarding how we might improve the product. When I visited these customers, they often remarked how impressed they are that Seiko Instruments remains interested in them even after their check had cleared the bank. Given this treatment, they feel comfortable coming back again and again to make new purchases.

If you ever have the opportunity to visit a Japanese supplier you will get an idea of what real customer service means. If you are the buyer, the customer, you are like visiting royalty to most Japanese companies. Arrive for your appointment and, more than likely, an employee will be stationed in the lobby by the elevator banks or even on the street, awaiting your arrival.

"Mr. Smith, we've been expecting you," goes the greeting, and the customer is feeling like a VIP—and the meeting hasn't even started yet. Many Japanese companies even have electronic signboards in their reception areas that announce the names and affiliations of the visitors who are expected on that day. But the most important thing is the fact that a friendly person, who already knows your name and is expecting to help you find your way, waits patiently, looking for you and hoping to be of service. In Japan, customers are treated more like visiting dignitaries.

Accomplishing this goal requires tangible investments of both time and money. In Japan, it is estimated that up to 5% of GNP is spent on business entertainment. I know personally of sales and marketing executives who have entertainment expense accounts of $10,000—per month! While recessionary pressures have reduced some of these expenditures, Japanese executives usually try to limit expenses in every conceivable area, down to recycling paper clips, before cutting back on the money they spend entertaining customers.

At Seiko Instruments, USA, we embarked on a journey to improve every aspect of customer service activities. The first step was to identify every instance in which a customer came in contact with our people. Events like customer com-

plaints, shipping and receiving activities, and customer inquiries were studied and analyzed. How long did it take us
to serve the customer in each instance? After determining
what the company was currently doing, we then set goals for
improvement, trying, for example, to cut in half the time it
takes to resolve a complaint, expedite an order, or answer a
question. Products are not the only thing we worked on
continuously improving. We wanted our customer service to
constantly improve as well.

Whether it is meeting visiting customers at the airport or
visiting them between sales just to see how they are doing,
the goal is always the same: strengthening the relationship
between customer and supplier beyond the needs of the
moment. In the end, success in business depends on winning customer loyalty at every opportunity. Financial investments aimed at improving customer service are important,
but the attitude of employees is equally vital. As in other
areas, I've learned that the Japanese culture and language
offer some vital insights into how these tasks can best be
accomplished.

Getting Ahead by Putting Others First

In Japan, the most sophisticated customer service techniques are based on a concept known as *omoiyari*, considered
one of the preferred and most virtuous forms of social interaction. In English, the practice might be translated as "filling
anticipated needs" but it really is much more than that. It is,
first and foremost, an attitude that combines both generosity
and altruism.

The omoiyari attitude places the needs of others first.
Rather than simply responding to a customer's needs, a
sense of omoiyari requires anticipating those needs. A sense
of omoiyari creates, for example, the mind-set that leads a

Japanese associate to call a taxi for a departing visitor before being asked, or assemble needed documents ahead of time, or, in a social setting, select a restaurant or bar that caters to the taste of the other person. While Westerners practice a good deal of this kind of consideration, the Japanese have taken it to a much higher level. The result is yet another enhancement of the strong interpersonal ties that create the atmosphere of trust in which business can then flourish. By constantly anticipating the needs of others, an individual, in the Japanese setting, becomes a leader.

Omoiyari shapes Japanese attitudes toward customer service. For example, a friend who travels to Japan about as often as I do noticed a slight but important omoiyari difference in the in-flight service offered by Japanese airline JAL and the popular American carriers. "On JAL, the stewards are trained to walk around the plane constantly offering coffee to the passengers," he notes. On the American carriers, "the coffee is just as good, but you have to ask for it." The Japanese omoiyari business practice is to anticipate what the passenger might want and provide it ahead of time. The American airlines' approach of accommodating customer requests is adequate, but rarely leaves the customer with the pampered feeling one gets on JAL.

This routine Japanese approach to customer service is quite impressive. Another example: I have a friend who once notified a Japanese-owned hotel in Hong Kong that he would arrive one day later than planned. Upon his late arrival at the hotel he was greeted by a fax that had arrived a day earlier, from one of his upcoming business appointments. It urgently requested a rescheduling of the appointment and a response that same day. The hotel staff, on their own, had already sent a fax back to my friends' colleague informing him that my friend was delayed and would arrive the following day. A copy of that fax was stapled to the earlier fax and presented to my friend upon check-in. Guess which hotel my friend always stays in whenever he visits Hong Kong?

Similarly, a night out in a Japanese restaurant is a good place to witness another surface form of omoiyari. Rarely will you ever see a Japanese pour beer into their own glass. To do so is regarded as rude. Instead, a Japanese dinner companion usually indicates thirst by filling the glasses of those in his dinner party. I learned long ago that, in Japan, if you are thirsty and want more beer, the proper thing to do is to fill the glass of your seatmate, who will then automatically return the favor. Omoiyari means that others come first. Putting the needs of others ahead of your own is a commonplace social practice in Japan; it is expected to be reciprocated and is regarded as a noble and virtuous gesture.

The level of customer service that follows naturally from a desire to anticipate customer needs in omoiyari fashion is really quite noticeable. At Japanese hotels bellboys usually stand right near the elevator, ready to grab any luggage before the customer reaches the checkout counter. No bell is rung to summon the help; the help knows people with bags will be coming off the elevator and they wait patiently for the opportunity to provide service.

Enryo is another Japanese word related to this pattern of conduct. Roughly speaking, enryo involves considering others by restraining one's own desires. The Japanese word describes the need to avoid making too many requests. The reasoning goes that, if you have to ask for something, it must be a bother or else it would already have been provided. As whatever requests might be contemplated could interfere with the omoiyari desires of the other person, it is necessary, the Japanese feel, to put your needs on hold in order to first fill the anticipated needs of others.

This can occasionally lead to some embarrassing moments. I can recall one occasion when the departure of our group to dinner was delayed interminably while everyone avoided making a suggestion so as not to interfere with the desires of others. More often than not, however, such extreme courtesy is preferable to a more blustery approach. Customers certainly notice the difference, even if only on a subconscious level.

In its simplest construction, anticipating the needs of customers and going the extra mile to impress them with your dedication are surefire first steps toward improving customer service. In this respect, most non-Japanese managers and workers can learn to improve their customer service activities by understanding and practicing omoiyari and enryo whenever possible.

The Reciprocal Relationship

In Japan, practicing omoiyari and enryo often results in the creation of *on*. Like many terms used in the conduct of business in Japan, on has no direct English translation. Roughly speaking, it can be understood as a form of reciprocal obligation, a loyalty that grows out of a business relationship, similar to giri. Giri is the obligation to return the favor that arises out of a sense of on.

In Japan, on is created by the act of bestowing on another person something (goods or services) that makes recipients grateful and arouses in them a sense of obligation to return the beneficial act. Creating and respecting on is another good way to keep your company in an entrepreneurial mode. It helps recognize and honor the important human relationships that make business success possible. Good Japanese managers, like the successful entrepreneurs I know, understand the importance of these relationships.

I always encourage all my middle managers to cultivate on whenever possible by, for example, inviting their business contacts or key customers and suppliers to dine with them, play golf, or find other pleasant ways to build a subtle bond between them. This paid off recently when one of my middle managers got advance warning of an impending supplier price cut in time to briefly hold back a contemplated order. This piece of valuable information came to us because the supplier's representative felt a degree of on to my manager, who had entertained him on a number of occasions; our end-user customers eventually benefited from the lower price we were then able to pass along.

These lessons are not news to most entrepreneurs, who usually start their businesses with little more than their rolodexes. They often rely on the goodwill of the individuals they have helped in the past and mine these relationships for the ingredients they need to build their businesses. In a similar vein, most Japanese managers I know work hard at maintaining these types of relationships throughout their entire careers. Usually this results in an enormous arsenal of talent at a manager's disposal.

Creating on is typically the goal of the seller in Japanese business. Usually, the seller must extend himself or herself somewhat before on becomes reciprocal. However, extending oneself in hopes of creating on for the sole and apparent purpose of exacting some later repayment is viewed suspiciously. Thus, the degree of self-effacement and the quality or purity of the service rendered are what really helps create on. Creating on is also the goal of the Japanese manager in terms of the relationship with his or her employees.

The desire to create on explains why Japanese salespersons, visiting customers, will sometimes stand out in the rain all day if they have to, or endure nearly any ordeal, in order to provide good customer service. The Japanese understanding of human nature is that such behavior will be noticed and rewarded in loyalty from those for whom the sacrifice has been made.

It is precisely because of a sense of on, rather than being

part of some evil Asian conspiracy, that many Japanese will rebuff low-cost sales offers from traveling Western merchants, who are then apt to scream bloody murder. Why, the Westerners often ask, won't Mr. Sato buy our components if our price is cheaper than they get from their usual supplier? In the West, the lowest bidder usually gets the job. But not in Japan.

In Japan, the company or individual with the strongest degree of on gets the job. Yes, your price may be lower, Mr. Sato may agree, but 12 years ago, he will tell you, when our factory burnt down, it was Mr. So-and-So who stayed with us all that night and the next day helping salvage damaged equipment. So what if your price is four cents less per unit? It is the customer service that matters most.

Of course, Japanese managers do consider issues of cost and price. Most likely, in the example given above, the customer will soon find a way to report to the supplier, in the honne mode, the fact that competitors are offering lower prices. And together, they will work to meet those new price targets.

The role reciprocal obligations play in Japan demonstrates the long-term benefits of providing good customer service. Too often, in contrast, non-Japanese sales managers are forced to justify the amount of time they spend on a sale in relation to the profits that result from that individual contract. The focus should instead be on creating a sense of on with customers, who are likely to be so impressed with the effort that they would never dream of taking their business elsewhere.

By modeling the right behavior, carefully and consistently focusing the missions of their companies, flattening the management pyramid, and providing the best possible customer service, managers, regardless of the size of their companies, can emulate entrepreneurs. Doing so, of course, is the most effective way to compete with them.

Alchemist's Tool Kit #8
Thinking Like an Entrepreneur Checklist

AMERICAN/WESTERN	JAPANESE
Leadership values: Visibly enthusiastic Charismatic	Leadership values: Listen carefully to others and achieve group consensus and harmony
Manager priorities are: ROI Increased shareholder value	Manager priorities are: Market share New products
Stockholder priorities are: Increased stock value Company growth Company stability	Stockholder priorities are: Company growth Company stability Increased stock value
Customer service— generally responds to the needs of others	Customer service—generally anticipates needs of others

MANAGEMENT TIPS

- Make the start-up mode permanent by continually refining and communicating the mission of your organization to employees, customers, and the community.

- Focus your product/company against the outside competition. Use slogans to communicate this.

- Remember, we tend to judge ourselves by our intentions, others judge us by our actions.

- 85% of your management behavior directly affects the performance of your subordinates. Set an example for your employees. It all starts at the top.

- A leader's physical fitness is a direct measure of his or her inner strength.

- Serve your employees and customers first. Investors will be satisfied with the result.

- Flatten your organization. Cut out the middle managers who merely broker information.

- Change your organizational span of control from the conventional 8 or 9 to 10 to 15 people. This will cut back on the need for middle manager positions.

- Customer service is everything. Make the customer the royalty of your company. Make frequent and consistent customer visits an MBO and responsibility of all senior managers.

- Turn routine operations like telephone technical support into proactive customer listening opportunities.

- Thank customers at every opportunity. Put a thank you note in your shipments. Call to thank customers for their business and, at the same time, ask how you can improve.

- Understand omoiyari. Get ahead in customer service by anticipating other people's needs rather than just responding to their requests.

- Create a sense of on—mutual obligation—among your customers, vendors, and colleagues by going the extra mile, especially when it is not required.

9

MARATHON MANAGEMENT:
Building Products and Markets

Marathon Management

Applying all the techniques mentioned in this book, important as they are, will not by itself guarantee the long-term success of your business. However, doing so should provide at least one essential advantage: keeping you in business long enough to develop a stream of quality products and build your company's global market share. Business has more in common with a marathon race than with any of the other sports competitions to which it is frequently compared. Only unlike marathons, there is no finish line—at least, one hopes not.

The single most important goal of every business is to stay in business, to stay in the race. In Japan, this desire is particularly noticeable; selling the company or closing a division is, for the most part, very uncommon practice no matter how bad conditions get. Instead, Japanese employees and managers are usually willing to endure numerous hardships and personal sacrifices in hopes of outlasting both hard times and their competition.

This attitude can have its drawbacks. Japanese managers sometimes stick with a product or an approach long after it has been soundly rejected by the marketplace. Their thinking is: If we quit, we certainly lose; if we keep trying, we still might win. They employ continuous improvement techniques tirelessly and, sometimes, stick with a losing proposition long after most objective observers have concluded the effort should be abandoned. Indeed, few Japanese managers and executives could ever be accused of giving up too soon. On the contrary, they usually persevere, employing culturally based, time-tested strategies designed to insure prosperity in good times and survival in bad times. These market-oriented techniques build on the recognition that the ultimate goal is to constantly increase global market share by creating and maintaining leadership in product development efforts. Doing so depends primarily on some very specific factors.

Fortunately, my experience with Japanese companies coincided with the successful development of dozens of new products, both by the companies I have been associated with as well as by Japanese firms led by people I have come to know and respect. I have participated, at a shirt-sleeve level, in many of these efforts and have taken away some very important lessons.

Specifically, I have learned that how products are developed has a great influence on whether those products turn out to be successful. I have also learned the importance of doing business internationally by building and investing in global market share. These two activities, product development and global marketing, may appear, at first glance, to be beyond the scope of many line managers. However, the importance of these activities can not be overstated. Attention to these concerns is what enables a company to keep ahead of the pack in the global business marathon.

Sticking to the Knitting

In contrast to the well-publicized fascination with deal-making that seems to have permeated Western business in recent years, the sense of what has been called "sticking to the knitting" characterizes successful Japanese companies, especially when it comes to product development.

Most Western businesspeople I know, and particularly the Americans, simply love to make deals. The high-profile large salaries and jackpot U.S. executive payoffs of the 1980s further encouraged this get-rich-quick deal-making. Japanese businesspeople, on the other hand, are more accustomed to making incremental improvements in their businesses rather than, say, trying to buy their way into a new product area by acquiring a company.

In addition, because of their different executive compensation patterns, selling a company in Japan is not the lucrative proposition it sometimes is outside Japan. There are very few "golden parachutes" for departing top Japanese executives, especially those at failing firms. Instead, the success of these managers depends on how well they can grow their companies.

For these reasons, most Japanese managers tend to concentrate on very narrow objectives. They feel that familiarity breeds comfort, not contempt. Cultural factors may also play a role in this. Many Japanese artists, for example, pick a subject or a style and stick with it forever. Yoshiharu Kimura, a renowned woodblock artist, has done nothing but birds for 25 years; for 10 years printmaker Shigeki Kuroda has been depicting only bicycles and umbrellas in every conceivable permutation. By staying focused and by applying the technique of kaizen, these artists consistently improve their work.

It was the same at Toshiba. We continually questioned how we could improve our position, but always in the context of what we were already doing. We were never drawn off track, even when seemingly attractive opportunities arose.

In 1987, for instance, I was approached by an entrepreneur with an intriguing plan for a laptop computer with an Apple Macintosh base. He had a solid scheme for solving the complicated legal and technical issues involved. When I proposed this plan to top management, I received a polite but emphatic "no." Toshiba's R&D management people in Japan told me their mission was to be king of the IBM-PC laptop business. And that was that.

Toshiba, a quite huge and very financially secure company, did not want to dilute their efforts by going into another area. The company's Japanese leaders felt that distribution channels, software philosophy, and different user communities in the Macintosh arena were just too far removed from their main line of interest.

I've also seen the stick-to-the-knitting mind-set played out at Seiko Instruments. For more than 50 years the company has been one of the world's largest manufacturers of quality watches. About 15 years ago, the company decided to diversify beyond its relatively mature category. But instead of buying other companies or inventing totally new products, either of which it could have done, the company looked inward to its own production processes—those proprietary technologies and applications it knew best. It commercialized those production processes and now has more than 15 product lines ranging from precision assembly robots to electronic components and computer peripherals.

Seiko Instruments former president Ichiro Hattori explained the process: "The watch industry contains elements of uncertainty in that it is supported by a single technique, that is, the watchmaking technique. Because of this, we had long thought about arming the Seiko Group with nonwatch products and their potentials in order to ensure diversification of technologies." For Mr. Hattori, the company's big opportunity came in the 1964 Tokyo Olympic Games, when Seiko was selected as the official timekeeper. "Among the achievements brought forth," for the Games, "were various special race timer systems and record indicator displays. These technological developments bore fruit later on in the form of small printers, flat panel displays, and other products."

Wall Street analysts, in contrast, tend to get all excited when a big company gobbles another in an unrelated area. Japanese are more apt to ask, "Well, what exactly do General Electric's people know about network television and investment banking?"

Sticking to the knitting is a way of channeling energy. Big company executives know their companies have the resources to pursue distant sirens, so, too frequently, off they go. It takes a lot of discipline to ignore all those distractions and stay focused. But after a while the discipline becomes automatic. Some may argue that it is wrong to be so narrow-minded but the more focused approach is better in the long run. It takes the emphasis off making deals and puts it on figuring out how to sell more, bring costs down, gain market share, and add more value for existing customers. By continuously improving the existing product line it is possible to defend and extend market share, as well as build on the core competencies of a company.

It is in the development and marketing of new products where this approach really pays off most handsomely. At that critical stage all the careful preparation, hard work, rigorous analysis, continuous improvement, and team-building through effective employee motivation are combined. It is the moment when a product is prepared to leave its maker and meet its market.

In the Japanese high-tech scene the product development phase is usually the single most exciting activity; employees jostle for a spot in the high-status product development group which, after all, is responsible for insuring the company's growth and often, its very survival.

Joining Toshiba and agreeing to help lead the development of its laptop computer business gave me a catbird's seat on this process. One of the first things we did was to make the obligatory tour of the Toshiba factory where whatever product we developed would be manufactured. Over the years I made this little tour more than 25 times. We would all put on our funny-looking hats (a great symbolic equalizer) and march around the shop floor, inspecting all the machines, shaking hands and bowing, learning who did what, and meeting, or at least smiling at, the workers whose job it was to translate our ideas and plans into actual products.

At Toshiba, nearly all product-planning meetings took place at the factory. The strong symbolism created by making the factory central to the product-planning process reflected the sense that the factory was indeed the heart of the operation. In many non-Japanese businesses the white-collar crowd rarely travels into the blue-collar domain; a permanent and very destructive chasm often exists between those who design and market a product and those who actually manufacture it. That is not the way it is done in Japan.

When I would visit Tokyo, about four times a year, we would convene at the factory. As vice president and general manager of a $350 million a year business I was expected to attend most product-planning meetings. These gatherings would typically include four to five people from the U.S. marketing and product support organization, four or five people from internal international sales and marketing organization, and, most important, 10 to 20 engineers from the factory. Most of the Japanese staff, engineering and otherwise, held undergraduate science or engineering degrees. And many of those who represented the international sales and marketing division had previously spent five to ten years working in the factory. This cross-training facilitated communication and respect between the marketing and engineering divisions.

The Engineering/Marketing Marriage— How to Defend Core Competence

In Japan, the product development process is driven by engineers, not by marketing types. Unlike the common practice in many Western companies, where a marketing team draws up specs and the company's engineers then try to hit the target, Japanese engineers are usually expected to personally research market needs and competitive products themselves. These product development specialists do not have to ask the engineers if something is possible; they are the engineers. Seiko Instruments, USA, has reduced the customary Western marketing staff/engineering staff chasm by hiring as many engineers as possible—and placing them in the marketing department. This approach works very well when refining products or making incremental improvements as it allows the product development process to move along at maximum speed.

Nonengineering marketing types, often valuable as company visionaries, no longer have to worry about these smaller issues. They are free to concentrate on the big picture by formulating advertising strategies or conceptualizing revolutionary new products. This is a very effective and even thrifty strategy, demonstrated most clearly, perhaps, by what happened to the document copier business in the past decade.

In 1983 Japan's Canon Corporation eclipsed Xerox in global copier market share. At the time, Canon was spending $50 million a year on very narrowly targeted research and development activities. Xerox was spending somewhere around $565 million on less targeted R&D. Clearly, the total amount spent on R&D had little direct bearing on the actual market performance of these two companies. What mattered is how the money was spent.

Gary Hamel, a scholar at the London School of Business, has been studying Japanese companies for a number of years and was one of the first to document the core competence concentration of successful Japanese companies like Canon. While Xerox was busy spending a fortune on interesting and glamorous research in fields ranging from image-processing to speech recognition, Canon was busy figuring out a more manageable, and ultimately, more lucrative proposition: how to make a plain paper copier for less than $1,000. In fact, Canon was so focused on this task that the company, long a leading camera maker, initially missed out on the market for auto-focus cameras, which were first popularized by arch rival Minolta. By concentrating on Canon's core competence, taking pictures, Minolta was able to do to Canon what Canon was busy doing to Xerox.

Canon's successful targeting of the low-end copier niche is an example of what can be accomplished by having clear product development goals. To test the market, to determine if there was in fact any real demand for "personal copiers," Canon actually created its first low-price copier by temporarily, and artificially, lowering the price of one of its existing models. This allowed Canon executives to determine if there was sufficient demand for inexpensive personal copiers to justify tooling up for large production runs. When the cheaper copiers sold like hot cakes, the company knew it was on to something.

Canon's low-end copier product development team then

came up with some simple goals for their new product, things like price, basic features, and performance standards. In contrast, Xerox was busy preparing the lengthy specs for its new copier product, an amazing "document production center" complete with all the bells and whistles, including variable power supply switches and built-in staplers. Lost in their capacity to do more, Xerox forgot to do better.

Canon's global leadership in these markets can be traced to a few decisions the company made in the 1980s. First, the company set a goal of reducing its product development times by 50%. Each division was asked to record the amount of time spent on product development activities for previous products and then get the same job done on the next product in half the time. Regular management review meetings were set up with each division. Doing as well as last time was considered a failure. Doing twice as good as the time before became the standard for acceptable performance. By setting these high goals the Canon management created a situation that nourished progress in leaps and bounds.

The company went on to identify six specific technical areas in which price performance issues would determine market leadership. Again, the goal was to take leadership of the copier market by taking leadership of the core technologies necessary for copiers. At first, Xerox executives acted as if they didn't know what had hit them. More recently, Xerox has made a resurgence, which its leaders credit to adopting many of the management and product development strategies of its Japanese rivals.

Attention to enhancing specific product features is another way to build on core competence. For example, Toshiba's laptop computer's much praised "auto resume" function, the first of its kind, was developed in 1987 after looking at the way early customers actually used the product. It was a customer- and market-centered solution. Our engineers discovered that most computer users want to start work right

203

where they left off when, later on, they switch the power back on. So we added a feature that does just that, automatically bringing users to the screen they were working on before they turned their computer off. Simple idea. Powerful feature. And based entirely on observations our engineers made about how our customers actually used our product.

In nearly every instance, when developing new products the emphasis should be placed on sticking with what one knows and building new products that extend the utility of these products and the profitability of basic competencies within the company. These core competencies should then be guarded and defended aggressively.

For example, Honda Motor Company executives realize that multivalve engines constitute the core of their business. Honda makes more multivalve engines than any other company in the world. While Honda might subcontract windshield wipers or air conditioners, the company will close down before it ever buys another company's multivalve engine. By keeping on top of the engine manufacturing business, and even manufacturing them for other companies, Honda is able to keep ahead of its competitors. Compare that with a company like GE, which sought to increase its short-term profits in consumer electronics by eliminating proprietary manufacturing of many of its products, subcontracting that work to less expensive Asian manufacturers. It must have seemed like a smart idea at the time. GE's stock initially rose on news of the company's increased profitability. However, it wasn't long before the Asian subcontractors owned those business lines. After all, in the end whoever actually makes the product controls the market. Try selling something you do not own.

At Toshiba, this concentration on core competence led to a surprising move. In 1986, when many U.S. manufacturers of floppy disk drives were going bust, Toshiba decided to vertically integrate into that business. The reasoning was that computers were what Toshiba did. With suppliers going under, it appeared that Toshiba might have to rely on a restricted market. Wanting to be the master of its own destiny, Toshiba decided that depending on any other business for so vital a component of its core business was too risky.

A Western venture capitalist looking at Toshiba's plan to get into the floppy drive business in 1986 would have laughed. I heard about this investment, which startled me, while playing golf with some Toshiba executives in Palm Springs. They pointed out that for the cost of six or seven Palm Springs homes that lined the fairways we were playing, Toshiba would be able to strengthen its hold over its core business. Turning a profit right away was not as important as protecting their strategic position in the computer industry. They wanted to defend and leverage their core competence.

The company slogged along on the cost learning curve as it built distribution channels for these new products. Soon, however, they were doing 1,000 units a month, then 4,000 or 5,000 units a month. Today, it is a profitable business, with roughly 100,000 floppy drives sold each month in the U.S. market alone.

Similarly, Seiko Instruments continues to grow its core watch production business by as much as 10% a year. Although the company is taking losses in other areas, Seiko's top Japanese managers retain a fixation with the watch business. That is the core of the company's international success; if that is lost, all will soon be lost.

Determining exactly what skills, techniques, and processes are the core of your company is the critical step in the ongoing product development process. Subcontracting only those parts of your product that are not essential to that core competence explains how a company like Sony is able to stay ahead of competitors even when a particular product fails. Betamax, for example, was a colossal flop. But Sony's core competence—expertise in the charged coupling device (CCD), which had been developed over a period of 20 years—was soon transplanted into a range of other products, like the highly successful 8mm video camera.

Such an approach may explain why it took the Toyota Motor Company $700 million to develop the Lexus while General Motors required a $4 billion expenditure to create the Saturn. Toyota never lost, or ceded to others, the core expertise that General Motors, at great expense, has now recaptured. At Honda, a successful product development team is usually put back to work immediately designing a new product or planning for the obsolescence of the product they have just created. Management is always looking for a way to preserve and carry over the skills of the product development team.

To cite a slightly different example, when piano sales slowed down in the 1970s, Yamaha, one of the leading Japanese piano makers, retooled and started selling electronic keyboards, rapidly becoming one of the world's major keyboard manufacturers. "They didn't cry because the piano market was dying," Gary Hamel told a group of USC international business students last year. "Instead, they concentrated on the functionality of their products, not the product itself." They concentrated on music, their core competence.

Saving product development money by carefully targeting product development efforts also enables more generous expenditures in areas in which these investments can really make a difference. For example, one of the first things I noticed at both Toshiba and Seiko Instruments was an extremely high travel budget. Both engineering and marketing people are constantly on the move, but not to expected places. Engineers visit customers and go to trade shows while marketing people are constantly traveling to the factory.

In successful Japanese companies the marketing and engineering functions operate as one seamless entity. This constant interaction creates a high sensitivity to both market and engineering opportunities. For example, at the Japanese companies where I've served, we usually held product review meetings several times during each major trade show, such as the PC industry's annual Comdex gatherings in the United States. Remarkably, these meetings often include more than ten engineers who traveled from the factory, accompanied by representatives from both the international sales and marketing division and the American sales subsidiary.

No one person is sent to the show and asked to collect brochures and write a report about competitive products. Instead, a virtual army from the factory descends on the competition, touching, feeling, and inspecting every nuance of the competitors' products. The person responsible for casing looks at the cases of the other products. The person responsible for display design checks out those features, and so on.

At Toshiba, we would convene evening review sessions once or twice during each trade show, sometimes lasting a full five hours. The meetings offered us a chance to go over in detail the observations made by each engineer and each marketing manager, who would then refer colleagues to booths where important developments were taking place. Of course, we usually had our own booth at these shows. But the real action, as far as we were concerned, was always taking place at the other company's booth. That was our classroom. While constantly concerned with more mundane issues, like whether or not we were meeting our six-month budget and sales goals, we were always equally interested in learning what NEC or Compaq was doing. How could we compete against their products? What products would they announce and how could we stay ahead of them? At Toshiba, I learned to live and breathe this single-minded concern, to focus constantly on the market, on what our needs were and what we needed to do to stay ahead of the competition. We assumed everything else would follow from that. And it usually did.

While attending these trade shows over the years I've also noticed that Japanese companies tend to introduce more new products than do most Western companies. Japanese companies seem to regularly venture into and out of the marketplace with new products at great speed, learning all the while. Western companies, on the other hand, often do the equivalent of stepping up to the batter's box and saying, "Now I will hit a homerun over the centerfield fence." When the slugger comes up six inches short, he's a failure and the crowd boos and turns away.

Like their approach to suggestion systems, Japanese product development managers are willing to come to the plate and bunt, hit a single, or just make contact with the ball. The important thing is to be in the marketplace testing the customers' reactions to your product and seeking ideas for improvement. The number of marketing insertions equals, in a real-world way, the degree of market learning. Developing new products is, in fact, a little like shooting arrows at a target obscured by fog. Most of the time you can not see the target clearly. You never really know how a market will react to a new product. So the best way to increase your chances of hitting the fog-shrouded target is to keep firing arrows, one after the other. Piling all of your hopes on one single long drawn-out product development process is like playing roulette by putting your whole bankroll on one number. You might win big, but more likely you will lose your chance to stay in the game.

The Knitting That Matters Most

Determining the best price for a new or existing product is another benefit derived from the marriage of marketing and engineering. *Fortune* magazine has this to say in a recent article about the development of new products by Japanese companies: "The team in charge of bringing a new product to market determines the price at which the product is most likely to appeal to potential buyers. From this critical judgement all else follows."

This observation certainly reflects my experience. In Japan, product prices are usually driven by the observations of the marketing and sales force. This is another way the Japanese engineering effort is always grounded in the marketplace. Key suppliers are also brought into the process. For example, we'll bring a supplier in and say, "Look, if you can supply this part at this price with these features, we can increase our purchases from you by a factor of ten." By involving key suppliers early in the process we become part of their team and they become part of ours, equally determined to build market share.

At Toshiba America, once we started building a consistent business base, the discussion quickly shifted from emphasis on survival to emphasis on market share. Gaining, increasing, and holding market share is the most measurable manifestation of the tenacious stick-to-the-knitting mentality.

Indeed, market share considerations have dominated business discussions with my Japanese superiors over the years. In fact, while my Japanese colleagues have asked me to analyze market share and sales growth trends thousands of times, I have never once been questioned about return-on-investment figures.

Electronic Business magazine illustrated this important point when it reviewed the 1990 performance of the top 20 electronic companies in both Japan and the United States. The findings clearly demonstrate the Japanese penchant for building market share. During 1990, for example, the top American electronic companies were actually twice as profitable as their Japanese competitors, posting average net profits of 6% versus 3% for the top Japanese electronic companies. The American companies, however, made those higher profits on fewer total sales than did the Japanese.

Until quite recently, most Japanese companies were not terribly worried about this.

Instead, they are keenly aware that strong market share is, over time, a major competitive advantage. Development costs come down, manufacturing costs come down, advertising payoffs increase, and quality improves. This is especially true for high-technology products, for which quality, features, and reliability are key selling points. Studies have shown over and over again that high-tech customers are reluctant to switch suppliers once they have gained comfort and confidence in a particular product line. In addition, most of the marketing surveys I've done over the years indicate that many customers make buying decisions because of the popularity of a product, that is, its market share, rather than because of advertising. In fact, a large market share is usually the best advertising possible. It is also axiomatic that it costs far more to get a new customer than it does to hold on to the one you already have. The best way to retain market share is to retain customers.

Japanese business leaders usually regard market share as their driving force. Pricing decisions are based, whenever possible, on the market price that will lead to market share increases. Production costs are considered, of course, but since it is assumed increased market share will reduce those costs, the first priority is always on gaining market share and making the investment necessary to do so. Frequently, Japanese manufacturers invest substantial sums, money that non-Japanese companies might use for advertising or dividend payments, to gain market share by reducing end-user prices. Since the volume of production is what most directly influences manufacturing cost, the goal is to decrease those costs by increasing the sales volume. Westerners can argue that this approach, selling products at or even below cost initially, is unfair. But while Westerners are busy arguing, the Japanese are busy scooping up market share.

The focus on market share by Japanese companies is also

facilitated by the fact that these companies frequently carry very high debt loads and, consequently, are less driven by worries about quarterly earnings reports. For most Japanese companies, the main fiscal constituent is the banker, not the investor. The close relationship between most Japanese companies and their banks helps Japanese executives focus on the market share needs of their companies. As long as the debt payments are made punctually, the Japanese banker usually remains unworried over the kinds of short-term considerations that cause angst on Wall Street, such as "Did your company earn more this quarter than last quarter?"

The Japanese banker, unlike many Western investors, mainly wants a company to maintain solvency, meet its debt payments, and preserve a competitive posture for the future by defending and extending market share. Sometimes, this requires taking a financial hit in a quarterly or year-end statement that might have been lessened by giving up some market share through increased product prices or downsizing in some way. While some Japanese banks and their client companies have been forced to review this sometimes costly practice because of the recent painful recession, most are sticking to their guns. Market share is the last thing many of them will surrender.

Unfortunately, influencing these kinds of macroeconomic factors may be beyond the reach of most managers and business leaders. However, in the rapidly evolving global market, more and more international companies are following the Japanese model of market penetration rather than staying fixated on short-term profit positions.

To overcome this problem, it is useful, when proposing and selling a budget to superiors, to prepare two alternatives:

- Plan "A"—"Business as usual": a sales number and an expense level to deliver that sales number within the six-month budget period plus a resulting profit

- Plan "B"—"Investment budget": a spending and sales plan designed to grow market share in subsequent budget periods, up to two years out.

Obviously, plan "B" results in lower profits in the short-term. However, by emphasizing the market share-driven nature of plan "B," it becomes possible to "quantify" the value of investments in the market. This is a very effective way to build the consensus required for the short-term sacrifices that lead to long-term results.

Most long-term investors, of course, already realize the benefits of gaining market share. If these market share-oriented expenses are discussed with the financial community openly and portrayed as investments in the market rather than as financial losses, sophisticated investors will usually respond positively. A financial loss scares investors away; a careful strategy to invest in building market share can be a powerful enticement to investors. It is ironic that both of these actions look nearly identical on a simple company P&L statement. My boss at Toshiba would always say "A budgeted loss is an investment, an unbudgeted loss is a big problem."

The advantages of a strong market share position are obvious: Word-of-mouth advertising is increased in proportion to the number of people using your product; being a leader equates to being a winner in the mind of prospective customers and employees; and your product becomes the standard by which others are judged. Sometimes, market share even allows you to charge a premium price for your respected product relative to the competition.

In the long run, market share needs to be held with a strong set of quality and reliability standards plus good post-sales support and a fair price. This is market share that is "purchased" or "owned." Conversely, market share gained by artificially low prices is considered "rented" market share, with little or no long-term value.

Rented market share can, however, sometimes be a first step to owning that market share. This is a very delicate high-wire act that requires managers who are close to the market—and close to the manufacturing as well. Oftentimes, Japanese companies turn rented market share into owned market share by using the high sales volumes generated as an engine to drive down their production and distribution costs. If you have to make ten units of an item, the cost per unit will remain fairly stable. But if you are able to make and sell 10 million units of the same item, there is no end to the ongoing efficiency improvements and cost savings this scale of production can allow.

In addition, in Japan most companies routinely set regular goals for reducing their production costs. At Casio and Sharp, for instance, the company policy is to bring down costs by 10 to 15% per year, year after year. It is no great accomplishment to do today what you did yesterday the same way and for the same cost. Achieving a reduction in costs is instead considered a routine business objective. In the United States, some of the best big companies, many of them customers of Seiko Instruments, USA, have also begun to employ this cost-down strategy, pushing for regular reductions in the prices Seiko Instruments charges them for components and products.

Ideally, costs should decrease in a percentage roughly equivalent to the percentage increase in sales volume. If sales volume increases 20%, for example, per unit production and distribution costs should fall by about 20%. Of course, managers may not always meet this goal. However, working toward it steadily and incrementally improves productivity and profitability.

Not all businesses lend themselves easily to this constant process of cost reduction. In some cases, raw material costs, inflation, and other factors present barriers to major savings. However, in most industries, ranging from electronics to automobiles, there are numerous opportunities to reduce costs.

In other industries, where raw materials are involved, it may even be possible to engineer substitutes for the most expensive materials or processes.

Take, for example, the Minolta corporation. Like most camera makers, Minolta's first products were made with bellows fashioned from sheepskin. When sheepskin prices rose, Minolta's engineers developed the first synthetic resin as a replacement. Another company might simply have raised their prices. Minolta's leadership, however, was determined to build market share by keeping prices low and was willing to entertain any idea, even changing raw materials, to meet their objective. In the end, not only did Minolta keep prices down, the company helped create an entirely new industry.

In most industries, it is possible to achieve at least some cost savings, either by negotiating component prices downward or by technological advances accomplished through reengineering. Refining the manufacturing or production processes and streamlining front office operations are other areas in which major efficiencies can often be found. Finally, and probably most importantly, by shortening the manufacturing lead time, lowering inventories, and more carefully targeting the product development cycle, additional savings can also be achieved. The goal, though, is always the same. Get good at what you do. Get better at what you do. Be the best at what you do. Stay the best at what you do.

The Battle and the Battlefield

One of the oddest advantages Japanese business leaders have enjoyed in recent years stems from the fact that Japan lost the Second World War. At the end of the war, Japanese businesses acted like a frog who got suddenly tossed into boiling water and quickly jumped out, with a determined and single-minded focus on developing export markets in order to survive. Businesses in the United States, on the other hand, flush with the Allied victory, were more like a frog in slowly heated water; the subtle temperature change went unnoticed until the critter croaked.

The Japanese knew at the end of the war that either they would have to export or they would remain in poverty. Westerners have slowly come to a similar appreciation of the importance of export activities. Let's hope it takes firm hold before the West boils to death in a permanently addled economy.

The export orientation of the Japanese economy took root when its companies were devastated and even personal survival was often in question. The central goal of economic planners in postwar Japan was on creating and nurturing industries that could bring in foreign currency.

Little wonder, then, that Japanese corporations now dominate so many key international industries. It is not magic, not genetics, not guile, not trickiness, which has enabled this. They simply had no choice.

In the United States, on the other hand, the neglect of markets outside its borders is one of the most glaring failures of many American businesses. For example, while U.S. auto and electronics manufacturers often plead for government assistance and protection, until quite recently few of them have made the total effort required to really compete in global markets.

In almost every product area, the real battlefield, the one that offers a chance of genuine and enduring victory, is the battlefield in the competitors' backyard. In addition to offering an opportunity for increased sales volume, demanding foreign markets, like those in Asia and Europe, provide the toughest proving ground for American products. Learning what consumers in these markets want, and meeting those needs, is the best way to keep one giant global step ahead of the competition. In short, you get better in your home base by selling over there.

Indeed, one need not be a student of von Clausewitz to understand why modern American political leaders have worked so hard to keep military confrontations far away. They realized, of course, that where a battle takes place in part determines the battle's consequences and eventual outcome. This is true in business as well. It is far better for American businesses to fight for and win loyalty from foreign consumers rather than continually be pressed to the wall, defending their own market. Competition in the competitors' backyard, their home market, provides the opportunity to test and improve products and companies in an environment in which the competition is the toughest. And competing against the toughest competition in the toughest place forces a company to do its very best. In the end, of course, the rewards go to whomever does the best, whomever produces the best products at the best prices with the best system of distribution.

Rather than send high-priced lobbyists to Washington, U.S. companies should instead send more engineers and marketing specialists to foreign markets. Managers should seek to bring the fight to the other guy's turf whenever possible. Remarkably, for instance, until the 1990s many American automakers would not even accommodate the common foreign custom of putting the steering wheel on the right-hand side. How many Hondas would have been sold in the United States if the steering wheel was on the wrong side?

After the much publicized, and some say disastrous, visit to Tokyo in 1992 by President George Bush and executives from the American auto industry, leading officials in Detroit finally announced they would begin making cars with the steering wheel in the proper location for the Asian market. But obviously, this move came far, far too late. It should have been done well before American manufacturers ever attempted to sell a single car in Japan. Of course, no Japanese company ever tried to sell a car in the United States with such an obvious design arrogance.

Sensitivity to local desires in foreign markets is a hall-mark of a successful company. At Toshiba, for example, when we made the decision to enter the laptop market, the natural thing for Tokyo to have done would have been to create an NEC-compatible product. NEC, Nippon Electric Corporation is very strong in Japan. Their general operating system and standards are first-rate and emulating them would have been cheaper than any other alternative. From the Japanese domestic point of view, NEC compatibility would have been the wise decision. In fact, anyone coming into the Japanese personal computer market would certainly have chosen NEC compatibility in order to produce a clone product the market would accept. The easy way for Toshiba to go would have been with the NEC standard. And that is why it did not happen.

Instead, Toshiba decided to be a "brighter Blue." We knew that IBM was setting PC standards for the entire world. Potential customers around the globe were already comfortable with IBM architecture. So, after considerable study and reflection, Toshiba's leaders made a decision that has been made countless times by countless companies in Japan. We decided to go the extra mile, to compete head-to-head with the best in their own marketplace and to use the competition's architecture and standards to outcreate and outhustle them.

Outhustling and outproducing international competitors may require Western managers to substantially reshape the way they think about their companies. For starters, as the Japanese have proven countless times, in every area from VCRs to laptop computers, there is no shame in copying what the competition does, as long as you do it better than they do. Westerners—especially Americans—can no longer afford global complacency in this regard.

In fact, the longer Western businesses neglect foreign markets the harder it will be for them to protect their position in domestic markets as well. In most businesses, efficiencies of scale are all-important: If a company supplies the entire world, it can produce product in the greatest quantities at the lowest prices. Ceding global markets to others is slow motion suicide.

On the other hand, once a decision is made to compete internationally, it is certainly possible for more Western businesses to find success in overseas markets. Even smaller organizations, those without huge marketing budgets, can and should take advantage of this opportunity. If the Japanese have demonstrated anything since World War II it is that, for a motivated and properly trained businessperson, the world can become a very small place indeed.

International Sales and Marketing Group

The key Japanese business unit that has helped many once small companies like Honda, Sony, and Seiko turn into huge international powerhouses is the international sales and marketing group (ISM). In Japan, the average ISM is highly influential and important. In most instances, the president of a foreign subsidiary reports directly to the general manager of the Japanese ISM. And the general manager of the ISM usually reports directly to the top corporate leadership in Japan.

The ISM is responsible for global business development outside Japan. In essence, it buys product from the Japanese side of the business and resells it to international subsidiaries at a markup, which covers its salaries and creates a pool for investing in growth elsewhere. When Toshiba established operations in the United States, the ISM had money to invest in us. Then after we got going, the ISM took money from us and invested it in Europe and Canada.

Toshiba's ISM developed these funds by tacking on a gross margin profit of between 6 and 8% on products it bought wholesale from its Japan side. This created a substantial financial base dedicated to international marketing. The crucial significance of the ISM is that it focuses solely on developing business internationally and has the organizational clout to make things happen. In a practical sense, the ISM is responsible for all nondomestic inventory and bears the ultimate responsibility for all foreign profit and loss statements.

Senior ISM personnel are typically international in outlook and usually have had several assignments in foreign markets. Outside Japan, they are responsible for compiling research on markets, identifying product development opportunities as well as providing an informal channel of communication between the international sale subsidiary and the Tokyo home office. Upon returning to Japan, they often help spearhead the product development effort for the foreign market they have studied. The vast training and substantial company and international experience of an average Japanese ISM manager are powerful advantages in this process. The typical career path of an ISM manager looks something like this:

Typical Japanese ISM Salaryman Career Path

1 year training, including factory.
3 years in computer development engineering.
3 years as system engineer in domestic market.
2 years study for MBA in United States.
3 years in ISM in printer international sales department.
3 years sales in Europe.

3 years in international computer sales department.

3 years as assistant general manager of U.S. computer division.

3 years as section head of disk drive sales in Tokyo.

3 years as head of the ISM planning department.

3 years as head of computer products division in Tokyo.

3 years in charge of a joint venture between a Japanese company and a western company.

University of Southern California Business School professor John Graham explains that for Japanese executives international training is a basic skill, part of their pattern of personal development. Writing in the *New York Times*, Graham cited the example of Yoshihiro Ueda. "Consider for a moment how the Japanese prepare an executive for work in the United States. . . . English language training started in grade school. He [Ueda] watched a lot of American television and movies. He received an undergraduate degree in economics from Tokyo University, then eight years' work experience, first in accounting, then in sales. By the age of 32, he'd been sent to an American business school for an M.B.A. and then was sent back to the home office in Tokyo for five years. Then he was sent back to the United States to open his company's first office here. And most important, his company gave him five years to succeed [in the United States] rather than the typical American approach of one year [in Japan]." The Japanese take international business very seriously and they prepare themselves for it in a dedicated and thorough manner.

At Toshiba, the power of the ISM was never in doubt. For example, Toshiba never did develop an NEC-compatible laptop computer, although NEC remains the compatibility standard in the Japanese domestic market. That shows how much power Toshiba's ISM had: Foreign markets came first.

Because of the ISM system, I basically had two bosses at Toshiba. I reported directly to the Japanese president of Toshiba America, who approved the business plan and evaluated the fiscal period business performance. But I also had a dotted line—a very thick, black dotted line—to Mr. Hataya, who represented the ISM. Mr. Hataya was interested in long-term business development in addition to meeting the current fiscal business plan. So each of my bosses had a different perspective. One manager was looking at the current profit and loss reports and the other was taking a high-road view of product development, spinoffs, and global marketing needs.

This arrangement gave me the flexibility to subordinate short-term pressures to long-term market development. For example, if I wanted to invest current profits to expand the market instead of making a higher percentage profit I could always make my case informally to my senior manager in the ISM, who would then informally influence Toshiba's president after I made my formal presentation on the matter.

Although many of the largest Western companies already have international sales and marketing organizations, these organizations typically do not have the same power or influence as does the average Japanese ISM. Remarkably, in a recent *INC.* magazine survey of American manufacturers and service companies with foreign operations and sales between $1 million and $100 million, more than half of those responding reported that they did not even have an international sales or marketing department. In these companies the CEO or the domestic marketing department handled the international side of the business. This is very wrong-headed.

CEO magazine confirmed this problem with another recent survey, which identified the key factors for American success in the global marketplace. American policymakers might be interested to know that the U.S. executives surveyed, for the most part, skipped right over the traditional litany of well-publicized political concerns like closed foreign markets, restrictive trade regulations, and such.

Instead, the U.S. executives surveyed agreed that a lack of well-trained global executives was their single biggest problem. Their second largest problem was an unclear global vision. It is not surprising, then, that with few qualified internationalists and even fewer clear global business plans, U.S. executives often stumble when it comes to coordinating and integrating their business activities across national boundaries. They do not have the people, the American executives told *CEO* magazine, and they do not have a plan. In a country as diverse as the United States, with an abundance of immigrants from all corners of the world, this situation is more than unfortunate; it is shameful.

In Japan, the highly respected ISM division handles the training, placement, and rotation of internationally minded workers and managers. Within the ISM, research is conducted and decisions made about which markets to target and how much local market share is required for profitability. A clear global strategic intent is established and plans are formulated and implemented, coordinated with but highly independent of the domestic activities of the company.

For example, Japanese ISM divisions help determine whether their company wants to establish a beachhead in a given market, that is, aim for market share of less than 10%, or if the goal is to "storm the castle" by grabbing more than 10% of market share. Each strategy has different costs and promises a different set of rewards and challenges. Sometimes, establishing a beachhead is a good way to sneak up on a foreign market, generating at least some sales and gaining a reputation without attracting too much initial attention from competitors. Japanese consumer electronics products, like televisions and VCRs, are one area in which this beachhead strategy worked quite well. These Japanese-made products gained market share slowly at first. When the beachhead was secure, they then stormed the castle and put most Western competitors out of action.

In other cases, such as in commodity businesses like computer chips, a brute force rush at the castle might make more sense. In this instance, the goal is to immediately produce huge quantities of quality products at prices low enough to win immediate market leadership. In either case, it is the well-trained people in the ISM division who can lead a company in setting and communicating the proper strategy.

Many Western companies became quite large by concentrating solely on their own domestic market. But to be a world-class company today, to develop truly competitive skills, to create the necessary critical mass for product development, to gain rather than lose market share, and to maintain significant corporate recognition, at least 30% of sales must come from outside the home market.

Smaller companies, those with sales in the area of just $5 or $10 million a year, should also make this their goal. A company that is producing a product, any product, in these quantities and is not generating at least 30% of sales in foreign markets risks losing its domestic market as well. This is just as true for widget manufacturers as it is for television producers. In markets in which U.S. exports have been strong, like entertainment and jet aircraft production, foreign penetration of U.S. markets has been minimal.

In other areas, in which the United States has given up on foreign markets, like in consumer electronics, U.S. manufacturers have rapidly lost their domestic market as well. I'm often asked, when is the appropriate time for a company to start looking at global markets? My answer: quickly, right away, now, if possible. Otherwise it may soon be too late.

Understanding the role and functions of the ISM is a key to effective international competition. Creating and then empowering an ISM manager or department and embracing this global orientation are of paramount importance. The more authority given, or taken, by an ISM the more likely it is that company will achieve lasting success in international markets.

The single largest obstacle to success in international markets cited by American executives in the *CEO* survey, a "lack of global executives" trained and able to operate in foreign cultures, does not similarly handicap Japan. According to the *New York Times*, there are now "over 10,000 Japanese citizens selling Japanese products and services in the United States . . . representing investments [language and cultural training, tuition expenses, etc.] of more than half a billion dollars by Japanese companies." Without similar U.S. investments in cross-cultural training aimed at creating a new generation of ISM personnel, it is unlikely the United States will ever reverse its trade deficit no matter how many promises any government, foreign or domestic, might make.

The Personal Touch

One of the biggest obstacles to entering foreign markets is the perception that such activities are simply too expensive. Yet that need not always be the case. Even when costs are incurred, however, the expense of not doing so can be even higher. For example, a representative of a major Japanese truck manufacturer was stationed in Teheran, Iran, throughout the entire Iranian revolution. "We haven't sold a truck in months," the Japanese salesman admitted, adding that nearly every other truck manufacturer had shut down their Iranian operations. "But when they get ready to buy again, we'll be here to remind them that we stayed here, we did not leave, and we are going to be here forever if they need us." The Japanese truck sales manager did everything he could to reduce costs. He even moved in with a local family to reduce housing expenses.

This attitude, that foreign markets are important enough to sacrifice even some creature comforts when necessary, is commonplace throughout Japanese business. Many Japanese salespersons spend more time in airplanes in one month than their Western counterparts spend in a year. And often, the Japanese spend that time riding coach. In fact, some of the cheapest ways to do business internationally can also be some of the most welcome and productive.

One of the greatest international business success stories in America, for example, is that of the little known Molex corporation in Lisle, Illinois. Molex makes electrical connectors, parts for VCRs, and things like that. The company now sells more than half a billion dollars of their high-tech gadgets each year, with most of those sales coming in Japan.

Back in the 1960s, however, Molex was a mom and pop operation selling parts for refrigerators. Then Fred Krehbiel, the founder's grandson, decided to try his hand at international business.

But Fred Krehbiel's father, who was running the company, refused to give young Fred much of a budget. In that first year just $50,000 was allocated to growing the international side of the business. So Fred Krehbiel got creative. "I couldn't afford to put potential foreign business partners or sales reps up in hotels," Krehbiel told a magazine reporter last year. "So I had them stay at my house in our guest room." The move, born of financial necessity, paid dividends young Krehbiel never imagined. The people who stayed at his home and ate at his table became far better partners than any stranger staying in a hotel room and meeting him at the office. One business guest was even at Krehbiel's home when he brought his first child back from the hospital.

Doing business internationally requires building even more of the trust and familiarity that also serve to lubricate domestic business. And building that sense of trust need not be as expensive as you might think. The only requirement is that the emphasis be placed on nurturing the cross-cultural relationships required by the situation.

Fortune magazine recently illustrated the advantages of this "high-touch" approach with the story of Korean merchant S. H. Jang, who traveled to Japan on behalf of Sandoz Korea to meet representatives from one of their suppliers of raw materials. "Arriving at the offices late in the day, he and his colleagues were immediately whisked to a hot springs resort for a communal bath with their Japanese hosts, whom they had not met before. From there they proceeded to a sumptuous banquet, to be entertained by geishas who charmed the visitors with old Korean folk songs. Later, everybody retired to a small bar for more song, dance and drink. The following morning, as Jang and his bleary-eyed Korean managers sat down with their Japanese suppliers to talk about pricing issues, he says, 'we felt like we had been friends for years.'"

It probably will be easy to convince American managers to party more with their key contacts in international markets but why not go even further? Why not provide employees a financial incentive to entertain the company's foreign guests, as is done regularly in Japan through company expense accounts?

In some instances, American managers, following the example of Molex's Fred Krehbiel, might even be willing to invite a foreign guest to stay in their own homes on occasion. At a minimum, however, international assignments should only be given to employees who have a genuine interest in foreign cultures and people. Some Americans will welcome the opportunity to get to know foreign businesspersons on an individual level. Some Americans might even discover, as Molex's Fred Krehbiel did, that they and their children can benefit from in-depth exposures to foreign guests. In the final analysis, the gulf that exists between cultures, and between businesses operating in those cultures, can only be bridged by individuals who learn to respect and like one another.

Often, American employees and managers, seeking privacy for themselves and their families, will resist making any of the friendly interpersonal efforts that are required in order to really get to know their foreign colleagues, partners, or customers. These people should not be in international assignments. Doing business across borders requires a greater, not lesser, commitment to nurturing human relationships. Trust is all-important in business, especially in international business. Creating that sense of trust takes time and effort but not necessarily all that much money.

The most important thing a manager can do to enhance international business development is to find employees who really do enjoy working with and interacting with foreigners. There are many such individuals. Creating a genuine sense of family that stretches across international borders is well worth the effort. The personal touch is the most important thing. While an expensive banquet for a foreign guest can help build these relationships, just as often, less expensive pleasures, like a dinner at home with your family can be an even more memorable relationship-builder.

Alchemist's Tool Kit #9
Building Products & Markets Checklist

AMERICAN/WESTERN

JAPANESE

Marketing drives product development

Engineering drives product development

Number of products marketed is usually greater than number of products manufactured

Number of products manufactured is usually greater than number of products marketed

MANAGEMENT TIPS

- Stick to the knitting. Be the best at what you do, forever.

- Incrementally improve your basic core business. Understand that core business and continually add to it.

- Understand your core technologies. Build your competence with these core strengths.

- Encourage your marketing people to visit the factory as much as possible. Make the factory a real and symbolic part of your product development process.

- Engineering and marketing must work as a team; empower engineering to make product specification-cost tradeoffs. Move engineers into the product marketing positions; move product marketing people into engineering.

- Concentrate on defining your market and building a critical market share. It is usually worth whatever sacrifices it may cost.

- Develop and present two budgets: one to stay where you are, and one to increase market share.

- A budgeted loss is an investment, an unbudgeted loss is a big problem.

- Create a highly empowered international sales and marketing department as a separate P&L center.

- Competing in an international market makes you a better competitor at home.

10

IN DIVERSITY THERE IS UNITY:

The Western Advantage

Creating the Third Culture

In the future, managers can play a central and crucial role in helping the West's businesses recapture lost economic ground. For a variety of reasons, Western businesses, particularly those in the United States, are now very well positioned to reestablish their role as the undisputed leader in global business and commerce. This economic revival is not inevitable, but, as this book underscores, it is possible.

Japan, on the other hand, is still reeling from its recent successes. Unsure of which parts of their culture are responsible for that success, many Japanese business leaders now seem a bit lost, wondering why what worked just yesterday does not seem to work today. Some of them are also handicapped by the arrogance that too often grows out of success. In fact, in the roughly one dozen years during which I've worked with them, I've watched many Japanese business leaders gradually change. Today, many of them spend less time listening and more time talking, less time learning and more time lecturing. Success has changed Japan.

The West, too, has changed. Economic prosperity is no longer taken for granted. Westerners now know, painful as the lesson has been, that they must work for what they want—and they must work hard. Nothing is automatic. More so than at any time in recent history, Westerners are listening, trying to learn and hoping to recapture the material comforts once thought to be the West's virtual birthright. Economic hard times have changed the West.

For these reasons, the opportunity now exists for Western managers to take the lead in fostering an international economic revival. Workers and executives are hungry for change; they are ready for it. In Japan, however, there is still confusion about what is going on. Notwithstanding the recent Japanese financial contraction, there is no consensus in Japan about the nature of the changes that are needed there, either in the business culture or in government policies.

Despite recent electoral turmoil connected to a series of sordid financial scandals, the same politicians and interest blocks who have governed Japan, for example, will most likely continue to exert great influence over Japan's government well into the foreseeable future. The same economic strategies, the ones that worked so well for so long, will be tinkered with and adjusted. But they will probably change only marginally in the coming years. It took a devastating loss in a disastrous war before the Japanese were able to successfully adjust their culture to become an international economic powerhouse. While the problems Japan is now experiencing are painful, they are not equivalent in magnitude to those that forced Japanese business leaders to adopt radically new ways of thinking five decades ago. In all likelihood, it will take many years of sustained economic hardship before major changes are implemented within the Japanese business culture.

Indeed, in the natural ebb and flow of economic history it is normal for any one nation's fortunes to surge and then subside, prosper and then retreat. Greeks, Romans, Dutch traders, Portuguese colonists, English globalists, American merchants, and Japanese multinationalists are among those who have taken turns leading parts of the global economy. This natural economic tide washes over businesspeople, entrepreneurs, managers, and employees alike, creating opportunities for some and obstacles for others.

When looking at this history, however, one thing becomes very clear: Adversity is often the best breeding ground for later triumph. Few predicted, of course, at the end of World War II the enormous success Japanese businesses would eventually enjoy.

Today, Japan is a prosperous country. Despite the recent prolonged recession, most Japanese remain grateful for the improvements in their lives brought about by Japan's economic success. Most of them can remember when things were much worse. While most Japanese are still accustomed to working very hard, some of the top Japanese writers and social observers fear the toughness and total discipline that characterized Japanese companies in the postwar era have begun to soften. In increasing numbers, Japanese workers are complaining about being pushed too hard while the Japanese media has even coined a new term to decribe Japan's younger generation, *shinjinrui*, which translates as "a new race."

This has coincided with some difficult new realities in Japan. In fact, many Japanese companies are now experiencing the most serious difficulties they have faced since the end of the Second World War. Throughout the 1980s, with annual GDP growth in the 5 to 6% range and with abundant low-cost capital, Japan experienced a runaway asset inflation. More recently, a combination of forces, including saturated export markets, overheated real estate and stock prices, and a chronic shortage of labor, has helped burst what has been called Japan's "bubble" economy.

Hurt by a global recession that reduced demand for many of Japan's key exports, Japanese stocks have tumbled, losing more than half their 1989 value by mid-1993. Japanese real estate prices, which peaked out at an astonishing $300,000 per square meter in Tokyo in the late 1980s, likewise went into a free fall. Similarly, Japan's banks have taken a major hit. Unlike U.S. banks, most Japanese banks are big investors in stocks; Mitsui Trust, for example, owns 5% of Sony's stock while Sanwa Bank and Tokai Bank together own 10% of Toyota's outstanding shares. As Japan's stock and real estate markets plunged, Japanese banks lost as much as $120 billion in unrealized capital gains, according to one estimate.

Like a race car driver who cheers when an opponent has mechanical problems, many Western observers have welcomed these developments. The *Wall Street Journal*, in an editorial, even went so far as to suggest readers hum "a Hallelujah Chorus" that the United States no longer has to fear Japan. The celebrations, however, may be premature. What matters most right now is not what happens to and in Japan, but whether Western managers can make the most of current opportunities.

Clearly, the recent Japanese fiscal downturn will not in itself solve the West's economic woes. But the West does have an opportunity to address those challenges itself. Japanese setbacks alone will not make Westerners better workers or better managers; that challenge is entirely theirs.

In the end, as always, the societies that best combine the most effective management techniques, regardless of where those practices originate, will find themselves on the cutting edge of global business. In the West, strengthening businesses by understanding, adapting and utilizing proven Japanese management techniques will not be easy. However, if Japanese business managers have demonstrated anything over the past few decades, it is the feasibility of assimilating and improving foreign business practices. Given the West's

233

traditionally open culture, especially that of the United States which is by nature infinitely more flexible than is Japan's more homogeneous society, managers and workers should now be able to learn from the Japanese much as the Japanese once learned from us.

After all, it was a Westerner, American quality control guru W. Edwards Deming, who first introduced the Japanese to modern engineering and production techniques after World War II. In doing so, Deming helped create something of a third culture in Japan, one that was neither fully Japanese nor fully American. By the time Deming arrived in Japan, of course, most Japanese were already predisposed to lives of discipline, hard work, continuous improvement, and sacrifice. Deming's contribution was to provide the eager and motivated Japanese workforce with some practical tools, like modern quality control regimes and specialized mass production techniques, which took root in the war-torn country and helped create the Japanese economic miracle. The Japanese honor the contribution made to their economy by this Westerner each year when they award their nation's most prestigious industrial prize: the Deming Award.

That Japan as a nation was able to reverse its economic fate in one generation serves as a reminder of what is now possible in the West. The United States, in particular, is arguably the most logical place where the global third culture, which Deming helped spawn in Japan after World War II, can now move into the next phase of its development, aided by the enormous strengths of the U.S. culture and society. Indeed, U.S. businesses enjoy several important advantages in this regard. Unlike Japan, for example, the United States has no shortage of labor. In addition, capital continues to rush toward the United States, sometimes from quite unlikely places.

Ironically, while it does not yet approach the scale of a Marshall-type plan, Japanese investors are among those helping revitalize the U.S. economy in much the same way the United States helped the Japanese economy after the war. By 1991 Japanese direct investment in the United States totaled more than $120 billion, with most of the individual investments falling in the $0 to $50 million range. According to Venture Economics, Inc., nearly 40% of all venture capital invested in the U.S. computer industry in 1989 came directly from Japanese corporate coffers. In the electronics field, Japanese venture capitalists similarly provided roughly 25% of the total dollar investment, with substantial chunks of the money flowing to the high-tech sectors on both North American coasts; in 1989 almost 30% of all venture funds invested on the U.S. Eastern Seaboard came from Japan, while in California, Japanese investors provided fully 60% of these start-up funds.

As recently as 1991, before the recession took hold, Japanese direct investment in the United States continued at a fast clip, totaling $15.7 billion and comprising almost 50% of all the direct foreign investments made by the Japanese that year. While many U.S. business leaders seem to have lost their confidence, Japanese business leaders have placed heavy bets on businesses in the United States. Clearly, these investments, which have not been withdrawn despite repeated dire predictions by a host of doomsayers, represent the Japanese understanding that there are ample opportunities for growth in the U.S. economy. Japanese investors, perhaps even more than most Americans, realize that U.S. businesses are becoming hungry once again. Given the cyclical nature of business, Japanese investors expect an economic recovery and hope to profit from it, not be victimized by it. Interestingly, many Japanese executives are now more optimistic about the U.S. economic future than they are about their own. The United States is changing, they believe. Japan does not yet know how to change—or what to change.

The third culture, combining the best aspects of Japanese

and Western management styles, is, in fact, already taking firm root in the United States and the rest of the West. We are paying attention and are beginning to transform ourselves and our businesses. More widespread use of employee stock ownership plans, for example, or the institution of quality control circles and a newly found but long overdue emphasis on customer service provide evidence of this albeit slow but certain U.S. business culture revival. At long last, Detroit's clunkers are starting to fade into memory while orders for GM's new Saturn are now outpacing production.

Japan is changing, too, but even more slowly, restrained by a powerful shared culture that, along with its efficiency and technical modernity, still adheres to some old and quite unproductive patterns. The outrageous treatment of women in Japan, for example, and the general Japanese suspicion of outsiders are two crippling remnants from Japan's cloistered past that present major obstacles to future Japanese prosperity.

In these respects, Japanese companies are victims of their own previous success. When you are losing markets and money, as many major Western corporations have done for two decades now, it is easy to accept the need for change. That acknowledgment is harder to come by when, like the Japanese, you have been mostly successful. Japanese managers will probably continue to apply the management techniques that led to their success as well as many of the ineffective or counterproductive practices that were somewhat less noticeable during Japan's boom years. As Western managers apply successful Japanese management techniques while rejecting Japanese practices that do not work, like sexism and xenophobia, they will create the third culture's next plateau.

In contrast, many Japanese business leaders now seem more determined than ever to stay their course, sticking with strategies that are in many cases no longer suited to current market demands. Kaizen, for example, is now being pushed, in Japan, to unworkable extremes as managers attempt to continuously improve endeavors that would be better abandoned entirely. Unable to make the fast decisions required by these crisis situations, many of these organizations are instead busy drawing their wagons into a circle. Rather than bringing more outsiders into the top ranks of their organizations, many Japanese companies are instead pushing these *gaijin* (foreigners) farther away.

In addition, the increasing pressures in the maturing global economy are helping make life even more unpleasant in many Japanese organizations than had previously been the case. In fact, according to one recent report, it is now not unusual for some Japanese workers to put in as many as 120 hours of overtime per month! There is even a word in Japanese, *kuroshi*, which means, literally, "death from overwork." Some estimates claim that as many as 10,000 Japanese workers are now killed by kuroshi each year. There are currently about 50 kuroshi cases working their way through the Japanese courts, a number that may seem small but which, in litigation-averse Japan, is really quite remarkable.

Along with the deep-seated xenophobia and sexism that exist in an average Japanese company, these kinds of pressures may overwhelm many Japanese managers in the years to come. Unfortunately for the Japanese, changing these practices will be very difficult. They are not surface features of the Japanese economy; they are instead the modern ingrained Japanese way of life. As Japanese managers have found (and as was humorously portrayed in the film *Gung Ho*), many of their culturally dependent management techniques are strongly resisted by non-Japanese workers, as they are also being increasingly resisted by younger Japanese workers. Exporting products was no problem, but exporting culturally dependent Japanese management techniques is now an enormous dilemma for Japanese business leaders. Many of the U.S. companies, including banks and real estate operations, which Japanese companies took over in recent years are now floundering due to this problem.

The scathing observations frustrated Japanese business and political leaders make regularly about U.S. workers illustrate this concern. Many Japanese business leaders seem completely unable or unwilling to recognize or acknowledge the advantages offered by non-Japanese management practices. Many Japanese managers simply have no appreciation of foreign management styles and absolutely no sense of what works and what does not work. In light of recent Japanese success in global markets, the typical Japanese business leader today is at least temporarily convinced he or she is right and that the rest of the world, particularly Westerners, are wrong, inferior, and not worth learning from. This smug attitude, which infected and helped bring down the West's economy in recent years, is now slowing down Japan.

The high tide of Japanese managerial arrogance does provide Western business leaders, managers, and employees the same opportunity to excel that a previous generation of Japanese made such good use of. The West can learn what the Japanese do best and why, combine it with what we do best, and, in the process Western businesses can take the lead once again.

In reality and despite what they themselves may think, the recent success of Japanese companies in global markets did not occur because these companies are led by Japanese; they have no genetic advantage. They have succeeded because they were able to change and deepen their own culture, to adopt and then imbed in their lives and workplaces certain values and practices which, like W. Edwards Deming, came first from the outside. The famous University of Tokyo, to cite yet another example, got its start as a school dedicated to teaching European business accounting methods to Japanese students. One of the key strengths of the Japanese, at least prior to their becoming swollen with success, has been a willingness, most noticeable when they were under extreme pressure, to understand, learn, and adapt foreign business practices to their own culture.

The same opportunity, the chance to deepen and improve business cultures without abandoning the best parts of national identities, now awaits a new generation of Western managers. The economic future belongs to those organizations, wherever they are located, which most successfully nurture the development of this third management culture.

Westerners, particularly Americans, have another, albeit unusual, strategic advantage: Westerners have become the underdogs. By taking advantage of the underdog's opportunity to learn from the competition, while not abandoning personal strengths, Westerners can alchemically create an economic culture that, like a new alloy, takes on strength greater than any of its individual components. Western managers who augment successful Japanese management techniques with some basic Western sensibilities will not only catch up with their Japanese competitors; they will be able to surpass them. Managers in countries other than Japan or the United States would do well to emulate and combine the best aspects of both the U.S. and Japanese methods of doing business.

The United States, beset as it is by numerous social problems, ranging from drug abuse to rising teen gang warfare to what seems to be a near permanent impoverished, untrained underclass, can best address these problems only if there is a sound and vibrant national economy. In the end, there is only so much government can do. If the United States is to succeed, the country's managers and workers must establish a new workplace culture that draws the best out of everyone.

What appears to many, including some Japanese leaders, to be the U.S. hodgepodge of conflicting ethnic interests and jangling social discord is in reality a most important strategic advantage: These are the raw material, the people, the descendants of the "huddled masses," and those who have just arrived, who represent an unparalleled and still largely untapped human resource. As Joel Kotkin and Yoriko Kishimoto noted in their book, *The Third Century: America's Resurgence in the Asian Era,* "In sharp contrast to both Japan and Europe, the United States is blessed by a diversity perhaps unprecedented in world history." Japanese leaders often deride this diversity and point to it as a problem. With better, smarter, more holistic management, however, the diverse population in the United States can soon reestablish the West's global economic leadership.

INDEX

A

Accountemps, 58
Aggressive patience, 145–49, 153
Aizuchi, 131
Alcoa Aluminum, 62, 64
Aoi, Joichi, 57
Apple Computer, 73–74, 171
Aspen Institute, 42
Authority, delegation of, 160–63

B

Benefits
packages, Japanese versus American (U.S.), 118–19
personalized, 61
as status symbols, 118
See also Bonuses, Wages
Blumberg, Michael, 111
Bonuses, 121
See also Benefits, Wages
Buddhism, 35
Budget
alternatives in, 211–12
as planning tool, 12–13
targets for, 15
vocabulary of, 13
Budget cycles
six-month, 10–22
12-month, 7–22
Bush, George, 216
Business cycles (planning)
six-month, 10–22
three-year, 18–20
12-month, 7–22
Business day, Japanese, 63–65, 99–100, 111–12, 176–77

and strengthening of collective identity, 77–78

Confucianism, 98

Continuous improvement. See *Kaizen*

Cross-training, 101–8, 111, 181–82, 201

Culture
American (U.S.)
individualistic, 79, 85
wide-open, 75, 234
and xenophilia, 75
Japanese
agrarian, 79, 149–50, 154, 155
and concept of *kata*, 36
and conception of time, 8–10
formality in, 129–30
group identity in, 40–42, 46–47, 54–55, 59, 74, 75–76
high-context communication of, 127
and *kaizen* philosophy, 27, 31
polychronic, 8–9, 10
relationship building in, 53, 58–60
and Shinto/Buddhist religions, 35
value of teamwork in, 86
third (blend of Japanese

and Western management styles), 234, 235, 239
Western
low-context communication of, 128
monochronic, 8–9
task-oriented, 65
workplace, 83, 84, 143, 178, 180, 239

Customer service, 183–92

D

Deadlines, 33

Decision-making
collaboration in, 158
communication in, 82
consensus in, 154–58, 162
in crisis situations, 148
linear versus circular, 150–54
negotiations in, 163–67
Western versus Japanese styles of, 143–70

DeMente, Boyd, 36

Deming, W. Edwards, 234, 238

Deming Award, 234

H

Hall, Edward, 67, 144
Hamel, Gary, 202, 206
Harai, Mr., 64, 67–68
Hataya, Mr., 221
Hattori, Ichiro, 75, 76, 77,
    198–99
Hidden Differences, 144
Hockey stick effect, 11–12
Honda Motor Company,
    45, 204, 206, 218
Honne, 62–67, 75, 138, 166,
    192
Hubris, 29

I

Iaccoca, Lee, 160–61
IBM, 43, 151, 155–56, 217
Imai, Masaki, 26
International sales and
    marketing group
    (ISM), 218–24
Investors, 212
Ishiguro, K., 181

J

JAL, 188
Jang, S. H., 226
Japan America Society, 184
Japan Development Bank,
    184
Japan Human Relations
    Association, 43
Japan's External Trade and
    Research Organization
    (JETRO), 171
Job security, 42
Jobs, Steve, 171

K

Ka, 40, 42, 183
Kacho, 104, 183
Kaizen (book), 26
Kaizen, 23–47, 74, 198, 236
    as competitive tool, 28,
    173
    as Japanese philosophy
    of life, 26, 27
    misunderstood as "quali-
    ty control," 26, 28